MELTON MOWBRAY

AN ILLUSTRATED HISTORY

Nottingham Street, Melton Mowbray.

PETER SMITH

ISBN-13: 978-1508916949

ISBN-10: 1508916942

LIST OF CONTENTS

This book is dedicated to my fried Peter Naylor, without whom it would not have been written.

Pete and I were sitting in the Boat Inn one night following a quiz talking about how many closed pubs there were in Melton. I wondered if it would be possible to do a map..........

Well, it was...one thing lead to another, and this book is the result.

Thanks also to Pat Traynor and John Smith for doing the proof reading. Any remaining mistakes are my fault!

I am conscious that there are modern photographs in this book as well as historical images.

Remember, though, that every photograph was new on the day it was taken,

and that history began yesterday.

CHAPTER 1

INTRODUCTION.

Melton Mowbray is a small market town with a significant history; for over a hundred years it was the haunt of the highest in the land and they left their mark on the architecture and the development of the town. Situated in the East Midlands Melton is ideally placed for getting to any other part of the country easily, but it has benefitted by being far enough away from the main routes not to have suffered from too much development. Now it is a quiet place again, known for pork pies and Stilton cheese but little else, but there is a big story to be told.

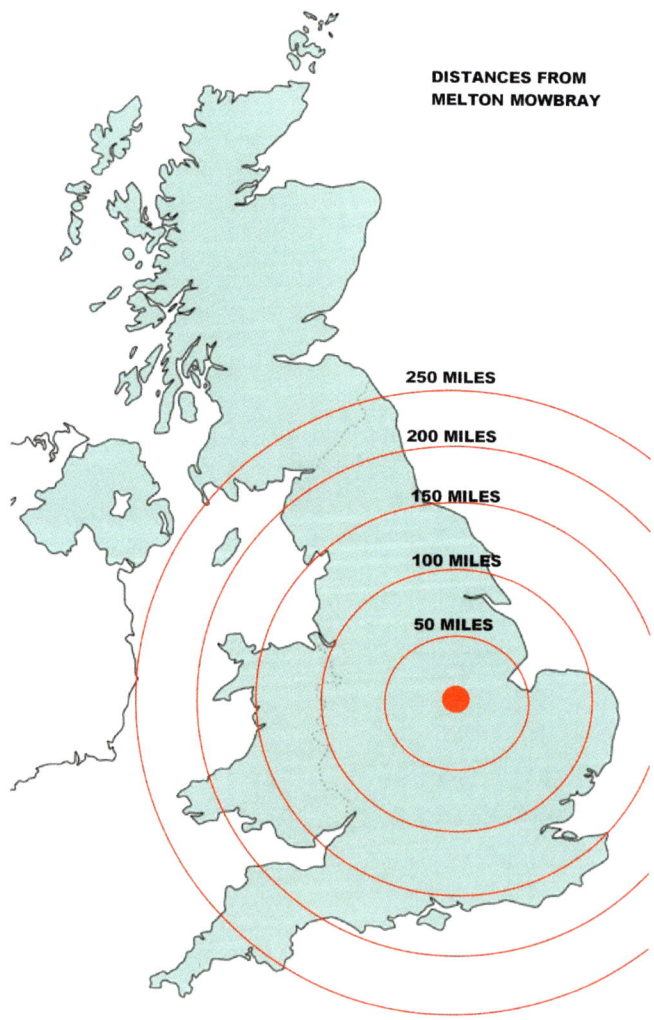

DISTANCES FROM
MELTON MOWBRAY

250 MILES

200 MILES

150 MILES

100 MILES

50 MILES

I came to the Melton area in 1981 and have lived here ever since; I can remember at the time trying to buy a book about the history of the town and being frustrated that the antics of a few aristocratic hooligans in 1837 seemed to be more important to writers then than the existence of the gas works, Wyvern Mill or the Midland Woodworking Co….none of those got a mention. In the ensuing years that hasn't really changed, but there is a lot more to the history of a town that just one night of bad behaviour. There have been books of pictures since then, but none of them really tell the comprehensive story of Melton Mowbray; the short captions simply don't allow it.

I hope this book redresses the balance, and that I have managed to find some photographs that you won't have seen before.

Winter in Burton Street in the 1930's; there were garages on both sides of the road
then, the pumps in the foreground are adjacent to the Harborough Hotel.

The pictures in this book, unless individually credited, are either taken by the author or are from the author's collection.

Tranquillity. The River Eye and Lady Wilton bridge in about 1920 with the church beyond.

Below is a similar scene a century or so before with Egerton Lodge on the left. This may well be the narrow medieval bridge that was replaced in 1820.

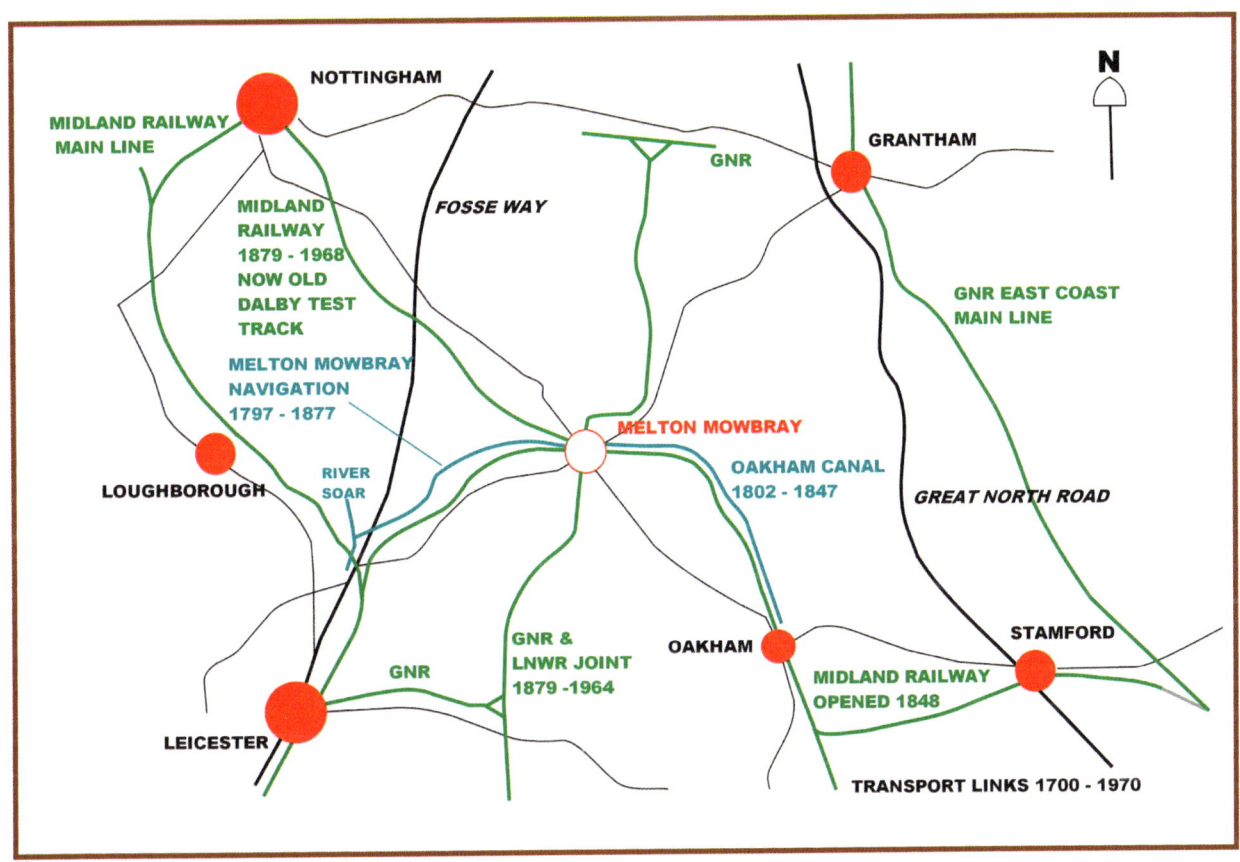

TRANSPORT LINKS 1700 - 1970

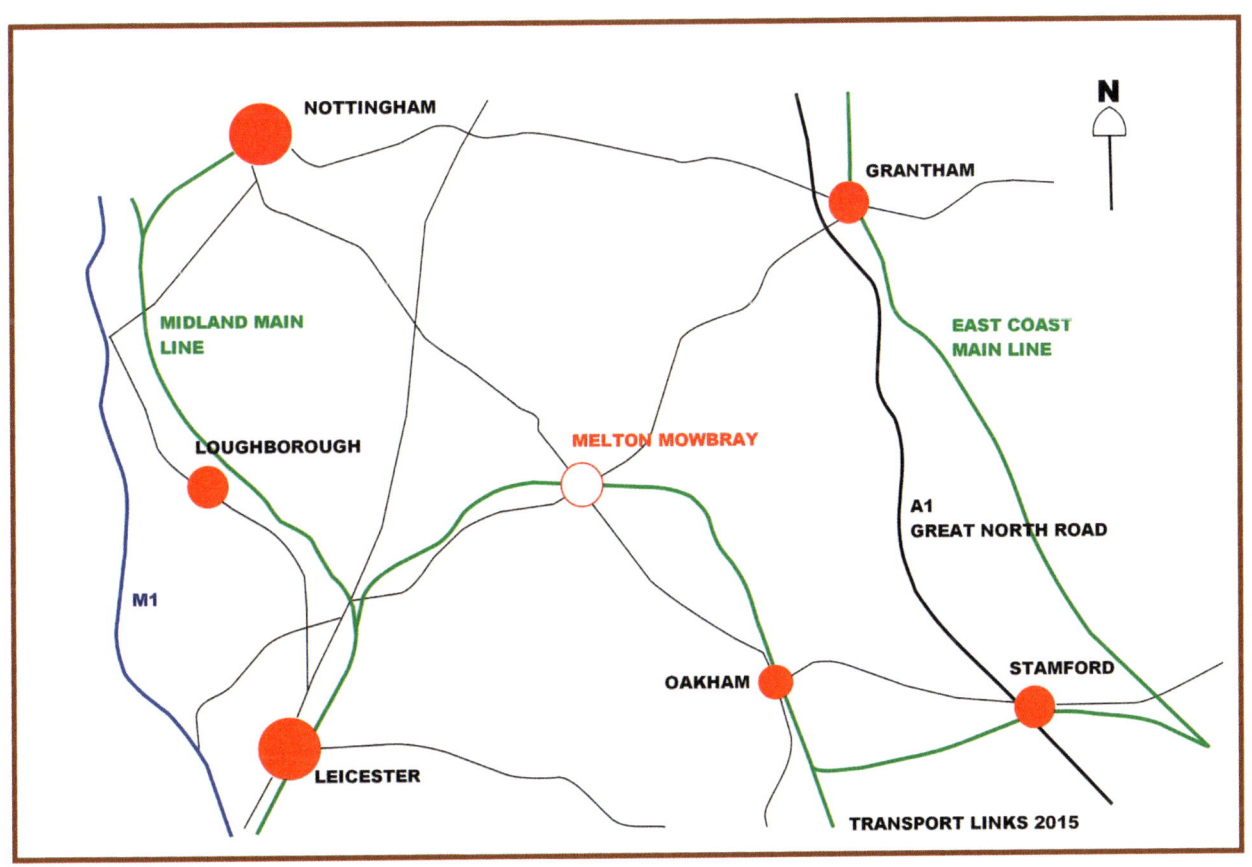

TRANSPORT LINKS 2015

Two wonderful pictures of Sherrard Street in about 1910. The top picture is looking from the market place towards Thorpe End with the old post office the right.

Below is a carnival procession passing the Granby Inn; there is a cast iron urinal on the right.

CHAPTER 2

MELTON FROM ABOVE

Before going back to the ancient history of the Melton area I thought it would be a good introduction to the book to share some wonderful aerial photographs of the town that were taken as long ago as 1926. Much still looks the same, but more still has vanished forever. What strikes me most is how few people are to be seen, not to mention road vehicles. The photographer was in a biplane, canvas covered and quite possibly not far advanced from those that flew in the First World War....the canvas covered wing can be seen in some of the pictures. It would have been a two seater, the pilot had enough to do flying the plane so a second crew member would have taken the pictures.

The town centre in 1926, the only part of the town little changed today nearly ninety years later. The market square has now been opened up by the demolition of the 'Barnes Block', and the far end of Sherrard Street has been redeveloped, but much is still recognisable.   Noteworthy is the lack of cars and how few people there are—compare it with a Tuesday in 2015! Judging by the shadows the sun is fairly low and in the south west, so a late afternoon time seems likely...perhaps it was mid summer and simply too hot to be out of doors.

Photo courtesy of English Heritage.

The plane circled St Mary's Church and took this picture from the west side; on the far side of Sherrard Street the Limes is clearly seen standing back from the road, a Jacobian mansion sadly demolished to make way for Woolworths. Little else visible on the far side of Sherrard Street survives today, but other than that much of the Melton seen here is still recognisable. Church Lane has changed very little and is arguably the most attractive corner of modern Melton.

This is Norman Street in 1926, looking east, and it is barely recognisable compared to modern day Melton. The court building at the bottom of the picture still survives, as does the cemetery of course with Chapel Street running along the far side. However, in the early 1980's Norman Street was converted into Norman Way, and everything on the left side of this picture was swept away. Norman Street was extended to meet up with Thorpe End which involved a huge amount of demolition and hasn't really done much to solve the traffic problems…..how much better to have built a proper bypass and allowed much of historic Melton to remain untouched.

The Wyvern Mills on Burton End in 1926, adjacent to the railway to Peterborough; Regent Street can be glimpsed on the left. The mill was on the site of the old water mill by Scalford Brook and was in turn replaced by the Pedigree factory which now covers pretty much all the land that can be seen. Melton gasworks is beyond the mill, accessed from the corner of Regent Street and Brook Street. The ring in the foreground seems to be in use as some sort of race track, perhaps for motor cycles....it doesn't look like an athletics track and is the wrong shape for horses or horse drawn vehicles. Allotments lie beyond it, and in the distance is the road to Saxby and Wymondham with remarkably little development compared with today.

Wyvern Mill is described in detail later in the book.

This 1926 picture taken from the south shows pretty much the whole town; the smudge in the corner is the wing of the aeroplane. In the foreground is the Midland station, and the Joint station can be seen in the distance marking the northern edge of the built up area. There is a large merry-go-round in the park with smaller stalls around it, perhaps a travelling fair rather than a permanent fixture. The route of the canal can easily be made out along the far side of the allotments, with the River Eye running across the lower left corner.

Photo courtesy of English Heritage.

PHOTOGRAPHS TAKEN IN 1953.

The town in 1953, with the Church in the centre bottom with Burton Street to the right of it. Wilton Road has been constructed and can be seen on the left, and top left there is a lot of new building off Nottingham Road. The fair is in town again, making use of Play Close.

Photo courtesy of English Heritage.

A second picture dating from 1953, looking East with Wilton Road at the bottom of the picture with the bus station and the school to the left of it. Barton's bus garage is on the site where the college & theatre now stands. It is interesting to follow the route carved through the town by Norman Way from the roundabout bottom left.

Photo courtesy of English Heritage.

CHAPTER 3

PREHISTORY, THE ROMANS AND THE SAXON PERIOD.

This chapter deals largely with a time when Melton Mowbray didn't exist, but an understanding of the time before the town was established is necessary in order to appreciate how it came to develop in late Saxon times.

The first evidence we have of people living in the area is the iron age hill fort at Burrough Hill, seven miles to the south of Melton. Standing 660 feet above sea level, this was a perfect defensive position with wide ranging views across the Wreake valley. Evidence suggests that the hill fort was first settled in the early iron age period and continued to be inhabited right up to the Medieval period after which it was used for farmland with ridge and furrow traces still to be seen. From the 17th century onwards it was simply used as grazing land.

Getting back to the early days, though, the fort probably developed as a centre for bronze and iron making, developing into the nearest thing to a town that existed then. The people would have lived in roundhouses similar to those recreated at Flag Fen.

They may look crude but they were weatherproof, warm and served people perfectly well for thousands of years. The area around the hilltop was given defensive banks and ditches but these were not forts in the way that we think of castles; they could be defended, but that was not the primary purpose. Apart from anything else the valleys were heavily wooded and often boggy, so it made sense to live on the higher ground.

Burrough was most intensively used between about 100BC and 50AD, up to the time of the Roman invasion, though it remained in use through the Roman period.

The Romans of course built the Fosse Way between Lincoln and Leicester and developed Leicester as a major centre. Six Hills was a camp on the Fosse, an intermediate stopping place for travellers and where soldiers could be based if necessary. Lesser Roman roads ran along the top of the scarp to the north of Melton, again because the lower ground was forested and swampy in places; the Vale of Belvoir had Roman settlements and roads ran to Oakham and Stamford. Melton, though, did not exist at that time.

It was not until the period of the Saxon invasions from the 8th century onwards that the first evidence of settlement in the Wreake Valley emerges, mainly through the place names. The Danish suffix 'by' is common right along the valley and is evidence that all these villages have their origins then. Saxon graves have also been found in Melton, Sysonby and Stapleford, so the probability is that although Melton does not end in 'by' it was established at the same time as the market town for the local villages, perhaps becoming more important because the river could be forded here. The name Melton seems to be a corruption of 'Middle Town', simply the place in the middle of all the villages that served as a market place for them. The name originated as 'Middletown', or in old English 'Medeltone', and became shortened over the years, long before the 'Mowbray' was added by the Normans.

The four ancient stone market crosses point to the importance of the town as a market place in the pre-Norman period, each one the site for selling a particular sort of goods (see Chapter 5).

The Viking invasions seem to have little effect on Melton, though the East Midlands was very much a centre of Viking settlement. The town at that time would have been small with few if any stone buildings, but the beginnings of the present street layout would have been recognisable. The rivers would have been forded rather than bridged.

Following the Norman invasion the first written evidence we have is contained in the Domesday book of 1086. Melton was then a town of some 200 people, little more than a hamlet by modern standards. There were two water mills on the Scalford Brook, Melton Mill and Beck Mill, and a weekly market was held which has of course continued right up to the present day. The market is said to go right back to the time of Edward the Confessor and is the only one in Leicestershire to be recorded in 1086, making it the third oldest in England. Royal approval was given in 1324 but it was established by at least 1077 with tolls being collected.

In the time of King Edward the Lord was Lewrie Fitz Lewin, whose lands extended over a large area of what is now Leicestershire.

During the early Norman period the pattern of market towns and villages became established, with Melton, Bottesford, Waltham & Wymondham being the largest places in the locality at that time. Although none of the buildings in Melton go back to that period many of the stone foundations do, and the street pattern we know today was firmly established by then.

CHAPTER 5

NORMAN MELTON AND THE MIDDLE AGES.

Following the Norman invasion society was turned upside down; one of the first acts of the new King was to impose a Norman overlord in place of the existing Saxons. This was in order to emphasise that the world had changed and the Normans were very much in charge from now on; the Domesday surveys were another manifestation of the same thing. As far as Melton was concerned, the very visible change was the building of a castle just to the north of the Market Square where King Street is now. This would not have been a massive stone fortress; there was no Motte, or artificial hill, and had a large structure been constructed remains of it would no doubt survive. In this case a fortified manor house was built, and we are fortunate in that a very similar building survives at Oakham in a very similar position, just off the town centre.

OKEHAM CASTLE.

A building such as this could be defended if necessary, but it was principally a home for the Lord and a centre for administration such as tax collecting and a court. There would have been a main gate leading into the town, and a curtain wall as shown here with the manor house in the centre. Other buildings such as stables would have been housed inside the wall and there would have been a well, so the manor could be self sufficient if attacked.

This is what Melton Castle would have looked like, a stone structure with a long hall and living accommodation for the Lord, his family and retainers.

The first Lord of the Manor of Melton following the conquest was Geoffrey de Wirce, who came from Anjou and certainly spoke no English. However, he soon became settled in the town because he married a Saxon woman called Aleva, a niece of the famed Lady Godiva of Coventry. She had considerable wealth herself, including large areas of Warwickshire. In 1077 all the tithes collected in Melton from the market were given to the Abbey of St Nicholas in Anjou, the first written record of the market.

Whether construction of the castle began during this period, or if Geoffrey even lived in Melton, has passed unrecorded but the likelihood is that he lived elsewhere in an existing manor house as he had many other Lorships as well as Melton. Geoffrey does not seem to have remained on the scene for long as before the end of the century he had died and his lands were split between Nigel de Albini and Robert de Mowbray. The former inherited the Manor of Melton so if things had turned out differently we might be living in Melton Albini!

The Molbrai family were Normans who took part in the conquest. Robert had been created Earl of Northumberland by King William and when Geoffrey died inherited half his lands, but not the Manor of Melton. The family name was soon anglicised to Mowbray.

Robert wasn't a very loyal subject; he got into trouble rebelling against King William Rufus and his lands were confiscated and given to Nigel de Albini so that the late Geoffrey's estate was now whole again.

Things now took another turn because the son of Nigel de Albini, Roger, took the name of de Mowbray by Royal Decree as did his brother Hamo. Roger inherited the Manor of Melton and Hamo began the Belers family who gave their name to Kirby Bellars. So began the association of the de Mowbray family with Melton, and the changing of the towns name to Melton Mowbray.

It is probably Roger who first actually lived in Melton and he may well have begun work on the castle, but not before he had gone on the Crusades. When he returned he endowed a great many religious houses and began the leper hospital at Burton Lazars. The present Melton church was also begun in his time, so he certainly left his mark on the town.

Roger was followed by his son Nigel, also a Crusader, only he didn't have the good fortune to return home. He was succeeded by William who became a very great man during the reign of King Richard 1st who was hardly even seen in England and needed loyal men to tend to the running of the country. When Richard was imprisoned on his return journey from a crusade it was William who was one of the main instigators in raising the ransom money. Later in the reign of King John he was signatory of the Magna Carta and his seal can be seen on the document; it is now the coat of arms of Melton Mowbray.

It is known that both King Richard and King John visited Melton and stayed at the castle, the first proof that the castle existed then. Sleepy market town it may have been, but Melton was making it's mark on history!

The De Mowbray family coat of arms in the 13th century.

Coat of arms of Roger de Mowbray.

The Medieval Coat of Arms of Melton Mowbray.

The present coat of arms of Melton Mowbray, still incorporating the white lion.

William de Mowbray died in 1222, not at Melton but at Axholme in Lincolnshire, and was followed by his son Nigel who in turn was succeeded by Roger de Mowbray. He was Lord of the Manor for forty years, a considerable span of time in those days. He continued the building of the bulk of the Church and when he dies in 1267 another Roger took his place, this Roger being a parliamentarian in the reign of Edward 1st. He died in 1298.

I am not going to continue through the whole history of the family; suffice it say that they retained the manor of Melton for 400 years, and by giving the town it's name and building the Church and the castle they really put Melton on the map with visits from two Kings.

The family connection with Melton ended in about 1480; the daughter of John de Mowbray, Duke of Norfok, succeeded the tile in 1475 but died as a child, the last of the line. The estates were divided between the Berkeley and Howard families, both having blood ties with the de Mowbrays. The Howards became Dukes of Norfolk, and with that the ownership of the Manor of Melton.

This may be when the castle fell out of use because the Duke of Norfolk had no use for an old manor house in a small market town which he probably never visited. For the time being, the place of Melton in the centre of English affairs was over.

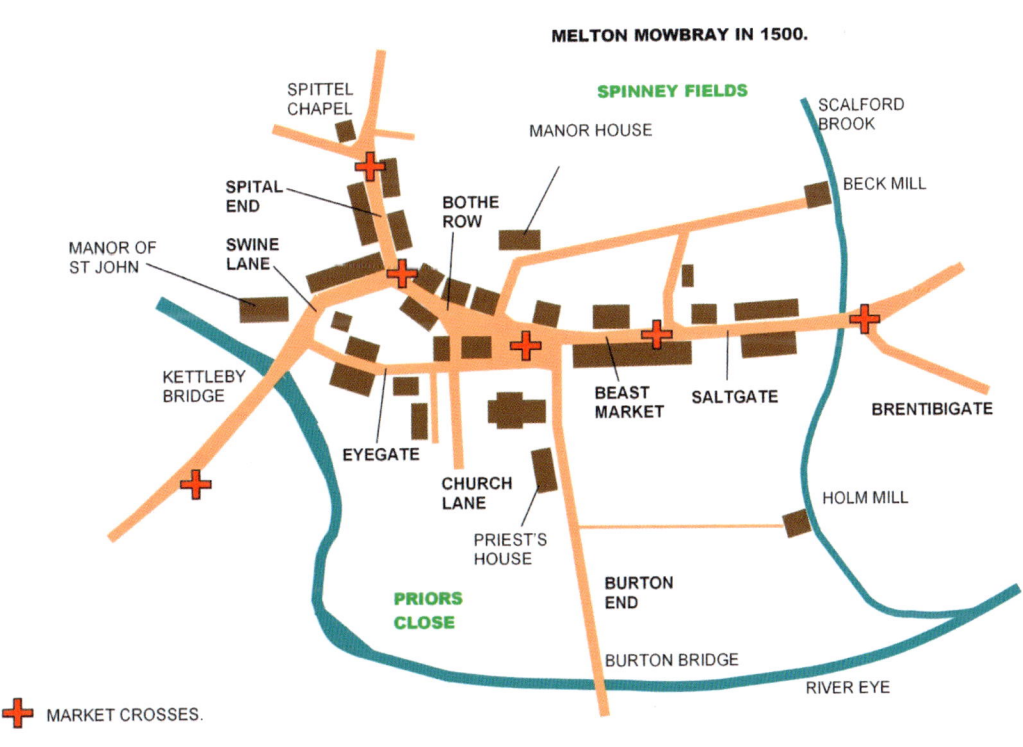

MELTON MOWBRAY IN 1500.

Very little remains of medieval Melton, but the Church and the Anne of Cleves, built originally as the priests house, remain much as built and would be recognisable to a visitor from that time. Other than the castle they were among the only stone buildings in the town.

The stone slate roof may or may not be original but certainly there were no chimneys in medieval times. My feeling is that it was probably thatched in the early days. Other than that, though, the fabric is pretty much as it has always looked.

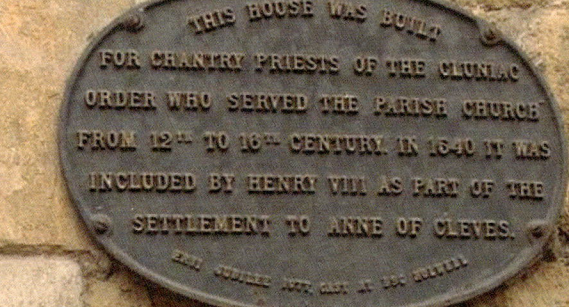

There is one more survival for those days, though you wouldn't think so from a casual glance. Number 5 King Street is a shop, but behind the façade is a medieval hall that is a remarkable survivor when you consider how much was demolished in Melton in recent years.

This shop began life as a 13th century halled house, and would have stood close to the castle at that time. The crown post in the roof was dated to 1330, and a record from 1313 states' Commissioner of Oyer and terminer to John Charnel and John de Cave on a complaint by John de Mowrbay, touching the persons who broke into his new house and carried away the timber'.

The map of 1500 reproduced earlier in the book shows a house on the same site labelled the Manor of John de Mowbray, certainly the same building.

It is likely to have been built with walls of ironstone and to have been single story, the roof timbers suggesting either a stone tiled roof or possibly wooden shingles, but not thatch. Two extensions were added in the 16th century perpendicular to the original building, the lower part of the walls in stone and the upper part timber framed.

The single story section was raised during the Georgian period and the roof was altered, and it was 'gentrified' with sash windows, a staircase, fireplaces etc. It looked like a very classy residence, hiding it's origins very well and all done far more cheaply than building a new house!

The Victorians added a kitchen extension, now demolished, and the early 20th century saw the final conversion, into a shop. So it remained until the end of the twentieth century, latterly as Manchester & Co. clothes shop, when it fell into disrepair. Happily the council stepped in and in 2003 the building was renovated and researched thoroughly; it is now open again as a shop, a wonderful survivor amid so much that has been lost.

With such an illustrious past, especially in the Medieval period, the thing that strikes me most is how small it is.

TRADE IN THE MIDDLE AGES.

Melton has no written record concerning the trades carried out in the town until the 1300's, but it is clear that by then the wool trade was already well established. It was in the centre of some of the best grazing land in England and on the edge of the great Lincolnshire wool growing region. A great council was convened at Westminster in 1339, in the reign of Edward 3rd, a trade council to which remarkably Melton sent three representatives. The wool trade was the most important of those under discussion, and Robert de Waltham, Robert Palmer and John de Brinkelo were chosen from among the local merchants (note that two of them still had the French 'de' in their name well into the fourteenth century).

There were many prosperous merchants in the town; one was John de Woodford, who was born humble but rose to become a rich wool merchant. He came to Melton in the early 1300's and married Alice Priest, daughter of one of the towns leading merchants and heir to his business—a good catch! By the time he died he owned half the town of Melton; he is reputed to have lived to 107 which would be remarkable even today, and he is buried at Thorpe Arnold. His son became a knight of Leicestershire, but later generations soon squandered his fortune.

In 1341 customs offices at Kingston upon Hull took half a mark for each 300 fleeces; Melton merchant Walter Prest was taxed on 20,000 fleeces! They were being exported to Flanders, and this was the largest payment of any recorded.

The Black Death struck in 1381 and records show that Melton was badly affected, with only 290 adults living in the town, making a total population of not more than 600, considered a small village today. Bear in mind that Melton was the second biggest town in the county after Leicester, though by 1563 Loughborough had grown larger.

The town did recover from the plague, and by Tudor times was prosperous again with wool still the main source of income. Right up to about 1800 the size of the town didn't grow appreciably, and most trade other than in fleeces was very local.

CHAPTER 5

THE MARKET CROSSES

There were originally four market crosses in Melton Mowbray but sadly none of the originals survived the dissolution in the time of Henry 8th and later road improvements. They were originally erected to mark the location for selling various goods, as a Medieval market stretched throughout he town and a marker point for selling cheese, for instance, was important, especially at a time when most people were illiterate. This method of selling actually continued long after the crosses had gone, into the middle of the nineteenth century.

The map shows the location of the original crosses; two have been re-erected in modern times, but not on the original site. There were also two crosses marking the boundary of the town.

The Sheep Cross stood in Spital End, now Nottingham Street; the sheep market was originally held here, then it was moved to Thorpe End where there was more room until the present market opened in 1867. Property owners could erect pens in front of their property not exceeding twelve feet into the road according to a statute dated 1700. The stone cross was still standing in 1577 but that is the last we hear about it; the exact position was probably in front of the later Baptist Church.

The Corn market was held on Cornhill, now the junction between Nottingham Street and High Street; corn continued to be sold here until the Corn Exchange was built in 1854 but the cross had gone by 1795. The modern replacement is in approximately the same position.

This reconstruction of the Corn Cross was erected in 1996.

Butter and Cheese were sold in the market place which is where the Butter Cross stood. It had an octagonal stone base which by 1795 is all that remained. This was also the High Cross, marking the centre of the town.

The reconstructed Butter Cross in the market square.

At the east end of Sherrard Street stood the vegetable and herb market and here was sited the Sage Cross, still remembered in the name of Sage Cross Street. Herbs were a vital source of medicine in those days, so this was a bustling area. This was the last cross the be removed; it was standing as late as 1870, opposite a house called 'The Elms' which is now the site of the former telephone exchange. In 1870, though, it was removed for redevelopment of the area; it seems a shame that it was not re-erected on another site.

These were the market crosses, but at least two others marked the edge of the town on important routes; they may have been others that have passed unrecorded.

The two crosses were Thorpe Cross at Thorpe End near the Wheatsheaf Inn and Kettleby Cross on the Leicester Road. Both had been removed by 1584 and the stone sold, and they were considered as being ancient even then. Thorpe Cross was sold for five shillings on condition that the buyer plant a tree in its place.

The cross on the Leicester road has recently been commemorated in the name of the new Wetherspoons pub which opened in 2009, a nice touch from a national company.

THE BATTLE OF MELTON.

The only time – as far as I know – that blood has been shed in quantity in Melton happened during the English Civil War.

There is surprisingly little known about the events locally during the Civil War, but Melton did play a minor role during which a battle was fought along with two lesser skirmishes.

Most of the local landowners were on the Parliamentary side in the conflict but three, Sir John Pate of Sysonby, Sir Erasmus de la Fontaine (glorious name!) of Kirby Bellars, and Henry Hudson in Melton town, were Royalists. The Parliamentarians, in spite of this, made Melton a garrison town.

The first meeting of the two sides occurred on November 28th 1643, a Monday morning, after the Royalist governor of Newark was informed that a group of parliamentarians were to visit Melton in order to assess the town for rates. Three hundred troops and dragoons set forth from Newark on the Sunday evening and entered Melton from Spital End early on Monday morning. The rebels were taken entirely by surprise and all were captured with only one man killed who refused to surrender with the others. The entire committee of Parliamentarians who had come to Melton were taken prisoner, a great embarrassment.

The second conflict did not end so easily. It took place over a year later, on Tuesday February 23rd 1645. The Roundheads had 2000 troops in the town, and a Royalist army commanded by Sir Marmaduke Langdale approached from the south west with 1500 men, along the road from Great Dalby. They reached the brow of the hill and looked down upon Melton only to see the Roundhead army on the far side of the River Eye, in fields along the road to Saxby. They had to advance through the town to meet the Royalists.

The royalist troops were all on horses, and being on the hilltop they were in a better position to prepare for battle. The two armies met in a field at the bottom of Ankle Hill, roughly between where the present leisure centre and railway bridge now are. The battle was short, and naturally both sides claimed to have been victorious. About a hundred men were slain in total, not a great many by the bloody standards of the time.

At the same time a smaller fight was taking place at Kirby Bellars at the house of Sir Erasmus, the old manor House that can still be seen there. A Royalist, he had been kicked out of his own house by the Roundheads who took it over and he was trying to win it back. Part of it caught fire and the conclusion was not decisive though again both sides claim to have won.

One mystery not yet solved is where the dead were buried; if a mass grave was dug it has never been found.

By the end of 1645 the Royalists had been defeated at Naseby and the Roundheads continued to garrison Melton Mowbray until the end of the war.

Henry Hudson, who lived at the Limes in Melton and was Lord of the Manor, was a loyal Royalist and once the Monarchy had been restored was knighted by Charles 2nd……..Melton used this as the excuse for a massive party lasting several days!

Before leaving this period there are two things that need to be cleared up, both concerning the street names in the area of the battle.

Ankle Hill is the road at the top of the hill that connects with Dalby Road and this is where the battle took place. Warwick Road runs past Warwick Lodge to join Burton Road at Burton End.

However, you wouldn't think so from looking at the road signs! As happened all over the country, in 1939 all road signs were removed, and remained that way for six years. Whoever got the job of putting them back up in 1945 got Ankle Hill and Warwick Road the wrong way round, and they've been like that ever since.

Secondly, the name—Ankle Hill. Rumour has it that it was named after the battle because it was ankle deep in blood.

It's a good story, and appealingly gory, but unfortunately it's not true, as the name appears in documents written long before the battle took place. The true origin of the name seems to be lost in the mists of time.

Burton Street, Melton Mowbray.

The Almshouses on Burton Street, which were the town library and museum in 1904 when this was taken. Originally built in 1646 as result of a gift from Robert Hudson, the Bede House was intended to house the poor people of the town. It became a museum in 1847.

CHAPTER6

THE EIGHTEENTH AND NINETEENTH CENTURIES.

At the beginning of the eighteenth century Melton was a small market town little changed from Medieval times, though new building in stone was beginning to replace the older wood framed buildings. Travel was only possible by foot, horseback or cart, stagecoaches and toll roads not yet having been introduced. The next two hundred years, though, would see more change than the previous thousand.

It was the advent of foxhunting in the eighteenth century that brought about the dramatic development of Melton, alongside the use of the town as a staging post for long distance coaches. This required Inns, hotels and stabling and brought employment and business opportunities. The first mail coaches ran in 1784 and the London to Leeds coach began in 1785, the first one to past through Melton, carrying most importantly the Royal Mail but also passengers. To modern eyes it looks dreadfully uncomfortable, which is was, but the alternative was walking or riding so in fact it was a huge advance which also brought about improvements in the road system.

The three big Hotels, the George, Bell and Harborough all opened in the late 1700's and the town began to take on a modern appearance though retaining the medieval street pattern. The opening of the canal right at the end of the century also brought benefits in terms of bringing in bulky goods such as coal much more cheaply.

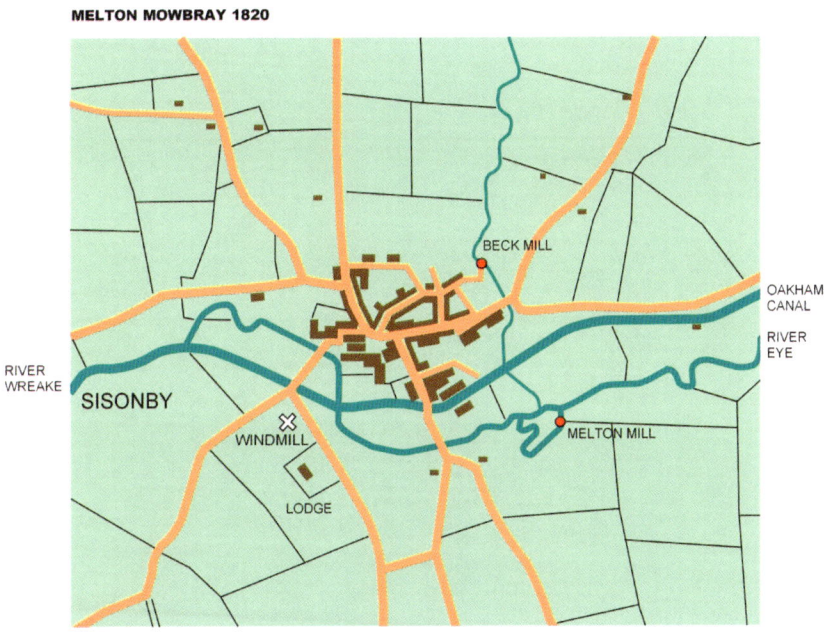

MELTON MOWBRAY 1820

In 1800 the town was still small, clustered around the market place but with little expansion outwards in any direction. The two Medieval water mills still ground corn for the town and there was a windmill at the bottom of Dalby Road. 'Sisonby' is not a mistake, it is the spelling in use at that time.

By 1839 some of the old street names were beginning to be replaced though there are some that we no longer use today.

THE TOWN CENTRE IN 1839

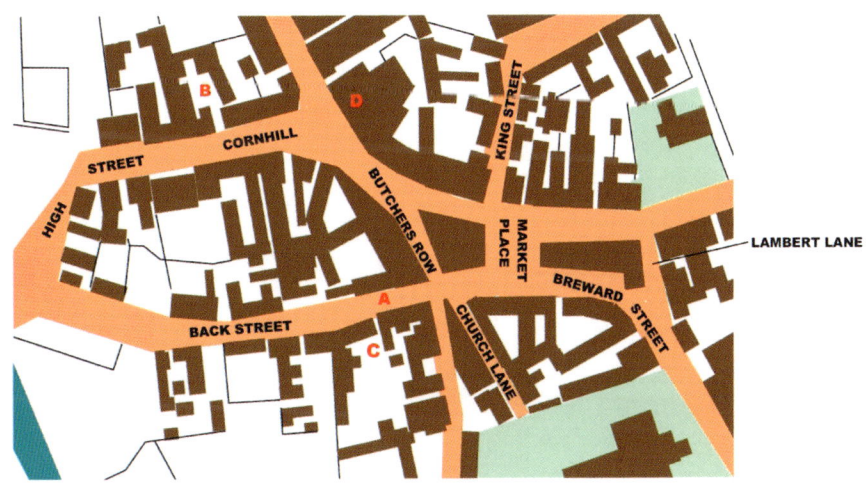

A - EDWARD ADCOCK'S BAKERY ON BACK STREET, HOME OF THE PORK PIE.
B - THE GEORGE HOTEL WHERE THE LONDON TO LEEDS STAGECOACH TERMINATED.
C - THE FOX INN YARD WHERE THE OMNIBUS FROM LEICESTER TERMINATED.
D - THE BELL HOTEL.

The earliest trade directory I have dates from 1827 and it makes interesting reading, dating as it does from just before industry really became established in the town.

MELTON MOWBRAY is a neat market-town, in the hundred of Framland, 106 miles from London and 15 from Leicester : it was formerly called *Medeleton* ; is situated on the road from London to Leeds, in a rich grazing country, and much celebrated for its being the residence of several noblemen and gentlemen of distinction, during the hunting season. The packs of hounds kept by the Duke of Rutland, at Belvoir castle ; by Lord Lonsdale, at Cottesmore ; and the subscription pack, at Quorndon, now hunted by Lord Southampton, afford the lovers of field sports an opportunity of hunting six days in the week : many houses in the town are furnished solely for these visiters, and some of the principal trades-people let lodgings to them during the winter months : there is also stabling in the town for five hundred horses. A court leet and baron is held every three weeks, for the recovery of debts under forty shillings, at which Jas. Thos. Bishop, Esq. presides. Lord Viscount Melbourne is lord of the manor, and Samuel Caldecot, Esq. is his steward. The church is a fine Gothic edifice, dedicated to St. Mary ; the ground plan is in the form of a cross, and the whole building is crowded with embattled parapets, with a tower rising from the centre. The living is a vicarage, in the patronage of — Godfrey, Esq. and in the incumbency of the Rev. Thos. Godfrey ; the Rev. Wm. John Shirkcliffe is curate of Melton Mowbray, and the Rev. — Brereton, curate of Freeby & Welby hamlets, in this parish. The river Eye runs close to the town, and is navigable to Leicester and Loughborough ; it also communicates with the Oakham canal. There

was no manufactory in this place till the year 1825, when one was erected for making Nottingham net, or lace, but only a few hands are employed in it. The town has estates belonging to it, which produce £700. per annum, which are applied in paying two school-masters and two school-mistresses, in lighting and paving the town; and for other public purposes : they are managed by twelve feoffees and two townwardens. A beed-house was founded by the Rev. Robt. Hudson, in the year 1641, for six poor men ; and the Rev. Robt. Storer left estates to trustees, for the poor of the town, the rents of which have been applied, up to the year 1827, in augmentation of Hudson's charity, by maintaining six poor women in the beed-house. The trustees of Storer's charity, in the year 1827, erected six new alms-houses, called 'Storer's alms-houses for poor people of the town of Melton.' The Wesleyan methodists and independents have each a chapel here, and there is a national school, conducted upon that liberal system that characterizes these useful establishments. The seats in this neighbourhood which give considerable consequence to it are, Stapleford-hall, the seat of the Earl of Harborough, and Belvoir castle, the princely seat of the Duke of Rutland. The market-day is on Tuesday ; and the fairs are, Monday and Tuesday after January 17th, for horses and horned cattle ; Holy-Thursday, March 13th, May 4th, and Whit-Tuesday, for horses, cattle and sheep ; and August 21st and September 7th, for cattle and swine. The whole parish contained, in 1821, 2,990 inhabitants, of which number 175 were in the hamlets of FREEBY and WELBY.

POST OFFICE, Market-place, L. Clementson, *Post Mistress.*—The LONDON Mail arrives at eight in the morning, and is despatched at four in the afternoon.—The LEEDS Mail arrives at half-past eight in the morning, and is despatched about the same time.—The BIRMINGHAM Mail arrives at four in the afternoon, and is despatched at nine in the morning.

NOBILITY, GENTRY AND CLERGY.
Artopp C. esq. Little Dalby
Artopp Rev. Wm. Evans, Harby
Bingham Rev. John A. Kettleby
Brereton Rev. —, Chapel st
Burdett Sir F. bart. Kerby Bellows
Barnaby Rev. Andrew, Asfordby

NOBILITY, &c.—Continued.
Palk Sir Lawrence, Little Dalby
Parkes James, esq. Sherrard st
Roberts Rev. James, Burton end
Skirtcliffe Rev. Wm. Jno. Burton end
Smith H. esq. Leesthorpe hall
Woodhall Rev. Wm. Braunstone

ACADEMIES & SCHOOLS.
Baker Miss (brdg. & day) Cornhill
Baker Wm. (boarding and day) Nottingham road
Everett Elizabeth, Sherrard st
FREE GRAMMAR SCHOOL, King st— John Brereton, master
NATIONAL SCHOOL, King street— William Coats, master
Wartnaby Misses (boarding & day) Sherrard street
Wilson Hannah, Sherrard st

AGENTS.
Judd John (to Commercial Coal Company) Canal
Wail David (to Hardy, Turner and Walkington, bankers) Market pl

ATTORNEYS.
Bishop Jas. Thos. Butchers' row
Caldecott Samuel, High st
Clark Thos. (& coroner) Sherrard st
Latham Charles & Wm. (and commissioners for taking affidavits in the Irish courts) Nottingham rd

AUCTIONEERS.
Burton & Clarke, Burton end

BAKERS & FLOUR DEALERS.
Adcock John, Nottingham road
Christian John, Sherrard st
Cunnington Edward, Sherrard st
Hill John, Nottingham road
Lord Thomas, King st
Lovitt Dixon, Church lane
Morrell Thomas, King st

BASKET MAKERS.
Whalley Mary, Spittle end
Whalley William, Sherrard st

BLACKSMITHS.
Adcock James, Sherrard st
Clay William, Sherrard st
Hicklin John, Sherrard st
Hill Thomas, Spittle end
Hinman Robert, Back st
Hinman William, Back st
Lineckers Abraham, Burton end
Lowden James, Sherrard st

BOOKSELLERS & STATIONRS.
Day John (& printer) Cornhill
Gilbert William, Market st
Towne John (& gilder) Market pl

BOOT AND SHOE MAKERS.
Adcock John, Church yard

Cleating Rev. John, Thorpe Arnolds
Day John, esq. Whymoodham
Day R. esq. Whymoodham
Day W. esq. Whymoodham
Faithful Rev. Geo. David, Eastwell
Greenwood Rev. —, Stathern
Harborough the Honble. Earl of, Stapleford park

CHINA, GLASS & EARTHEN-WARE DEALERS.
Caunt Wm. Nottingham road
Nichols John, Market place
Tuxford Wm. Thorpe (wholesale) Market place

CHYMISTS & DRUGGISTS.
Ellaby John, Market place
Howard Wm. Nottingham road
Kirk James, Market place
Pearson Robert, High st

CONFECTIONERS.
Norfolk Mary, High st
Pilkington George, Market place
Short Elizabeth, Nottingham road

COOPERS.
Bennett Thomas, Back st
Cavill Thomas P. Back st
Shelton John, Spittle st

CURRIERS.
Brett Wm. Nottingham road
Brown & Sons, Corn market

CUTLERS.
Bryan Benjamin, Timber hill
Webster Thomas (and gun maker) Sherrard street

FIRE, &c. OFFICE AGENTS.
BRITISH COMMERCIAL, Robt. Tyler, Market place
COUNTY (fire) & PROVIDENT (life) Edward Bright, Corn market
GUARDIAN, David Wall, Market pl
SUN, Thos. Henton, Market place

FISHMONGERS.
Dickinson Edward, Spittle end
Dickinson Guido, High st

GROCERS & TEA DEALERS.
Marked thus * are Wholesale.
Barker John, Market place
Boyer John Jackson, King st
Easom Wm. Sherrard end
Hawley Wm. Sherrard st
Leadbetter John (and druggist) Market place
Mayfield Thos. Burton end
Pears Wm. Nottingham road
*Tuxford Wm. Thorpe, Market pl
Walton John, Market place
*Wing & Sons, Market place

HAIR DRESSERS AND PERFUMERS.
Ares William, Market place
Rimmington James, High st
Short Elizabeth, Butcher's row
Simpson Joseph, Sherrard st

HATTERS, HOSIERS & GLOVRS
Draper John, Cornhill
Henton Thos. Market place
Hickson John, Market place
Scattergood Francis, High st

Hoe Rev. Thos. Long Clawxton
Hose Seth, gent. Sherrard st
Inett Wm. esq. Great Dalby
Manners Otho, esq. Goadby Marwood [Marwood
Manners Rev. Edward, Goadby
Noble Rev. John, Frisby
Norman Richard, esq. Sherrard st
Jelly John, Kettley

MILLINERS & DRESS MKRS.
Adcock Maria, Corn market
Allen Peggy, Sherrard st
Bass Elizabeth, Cornhill
Caldicott Harriet, King st
Draper Mary, Chapel st
Emson Sarah, Burton end
Lee Jane, Church lane
Porcer Alice, Corn market
Shelton Catharine, High st
Sills Elizth. & Frances, Sherrard st
Woolley Lucy, Chapel st

MILLWRIGHT.
Cooke Gideon (& brass founder and machine maker) Sherrard st

PLUMBERS & GLAZIERS.
Cole Francis, Back st
Mather Francis, King st
Nichols John, Market place

SADDLERS.
Allen Richard, Market place
Day Thomas, Nottingham road
Gibbs Fisher, Market place
Whittaker Thos. Copless row

SEEDSMEN.
Mason Robert, King st
Whitby John, Birmingham road

STRAW HAT MANUFACTRS.
Allen P. Sherrard st
Hill Ann, Burton end
Whalley Emma, Sherrard st

SURGEONS.
Darker Francis, Sherrard st
Fowler Thos. Nottingham road
Keal John, King st [ket
Whitchurch & Berridge, Corn market
Whitchurch Reuben, High st

TAILORS.
Marked thus * are Drapers also.
Daft William, Burton end
Davy Percy, Nottingham road
*Dewey John, Nottingham road
*Henton Thos. Market place
Hopkins John, Nottingham road
Kittle Henry, Timber hill
*Preston & West, High st
Swan John, Church yard
Wainer William, King st

TALLOW CHANDLERS.
Barker John, Market place
Pears Wm. Nottingham road

TAVERNS & PUBLIC HOUSES.
Black Moor's Head, Saml. Littler, Market place [rard st
Black Swan, Joseph Oldham, Sherrard st
Boat, Ann Brewster, Burton end
Bricklayers' Arms, Joseph Wakerley, Timber hill [road
Bulls, Edw. Bawderson, Nottingham

Hinman William, Back st
Linekers Abraham, Burton end
Lowden James, Sherrard st
BOOKSELLERS & STATIONRS.
Day John (& printer) Cornhill
Gilbert William, Market st
Towne John (& gilder) Market pl
BOOT AND SHOE MAKERS.
Adcock John, Church yard
Corner John, Church lane
Goodman Samuel, Sherrard st
Hickson William, High st
Jesson John, Sherrard st
Manchester Thomas, Burton end
Manchester William, High st
Marshall William, Copless row
Palmer Wm. Sherrard st
Thorpe Thomas, Back st
BRAZIERS AND TINMEN.
Cartwright Humphrey, Market pl
Manchester Edward, Butcher's row
Tebbs George, Market place
BUTCHERS.
Anderson Brothers, Sherrard st
Bagworth John, Spittle end
Cartwright Charles, Sherrard st
Harrington John, Burton end
Hawley Wm. Sherrard st
Mason Wm. Burton end
North Thomas, Queen st
Thorpe Wm. Butcher's row
Walker Thomas, Spittle end
Ward Thomas, Butcher's row
Whitle James, Market place
Wright Thos. Butcher's row
CABINET MAKER.
Burton Thomas, Burton end

TURNERS.
James John, Sherrard st
Langham Wm. Nottingham road
VETERINARY SURGEON.
Brown Samuel, Nottingham road
WATCH & CLOCK MAKERS.
Ellis Richard, Timber hill
Hallam Thos. Timber hill
Sharman John, Sherrard st
Tyler Robert, Market place
WINE & SPIRIT MERCHANTS.
Bishop Joseph (retail) Market pl
Hall Wm. (& brewer) King st
Peach & Brown, Corn market

Miscellaneous.
Baker Wm. farrier, Burton end
Brookhouse Sml. dyer, Timber hill
Dixon Wm. bricklayer, Timber hill
Hickson Jno. music seller, Market pl
Law John, clerk to the magistrates
and surveyor of taxes, King st
Neale Wm. architect, Burton end
Parker Thos. poulterer, Church la
Topps Wm. hosier, &c. Church lane
Tyler Wm. wheelwright & maltster,
Nottingham road
Willis Wm. collector for the Oak-
ham Canal Co. Burton end
Wyles John, painter, Back st

COACHES.
To LONDON, the Royal Mail (from
Leeds) calls at the George, at eight in
the morning; goes thro' Oakham, Up-
pingham, Bedford and Barnet.
To BIRMINGHAM, the Royal Mail
(from Stamford, calls at the George, at
nine in the morning; goes thro' Leicester, Hinckley, Nuneaton and Coventry.
To CAMBRIDGE, the Alexander (from
Leicester) calls at the George, every
Tuesday, Thursday and Saturday at
nine in the morning; goes thro' Stamford, Stilton and Huntington.
To GRANTHAM, the Champion (from
Leicester) calls at the Fox, every Tues.
Thurs. and Saturday, at six in the even.
To LEEDS, the Royal Mail (from London)
calls at the George, every morning at a
quarter past eight; goes through Nottingham, Mansfield, Chesterfield, Shef-
field, Barnsley and Wakefield.

Ares William, Market place
Rimmington James, High st
Short Elizabeth, Butcher's row
Simpson Joseph, Sherrard st
HATTERS, HOSIERS & GLOVRS
Draper John, Cornhill
Henton Thos. Market place
Hickson John, Market place
Scattergood Francis, High st
INNS.
Bell & Swan, John Sharp, Corn mkt
George, John Daniel Fryatt, High st
IRONMONGERS.
Bright Edward (& oil & colourman)
Corn market
Sharman John, Sherrard st
Tyler Rbt. (& silversmth) Market pl
JOINERS AND CARPENTERS.
Black Thos. Timber hill
Caldwell John, Nottingham road
Gray Sarah, Burton end
Sansom William, Back st
Shipley William, Back st
Steele Thos. Sherrard st
Worrall John, Ross st
LINEN & WOOLLEN DRAPERS.
Baker Thos. Market place
Brewin Thomas, Market place
Judd Robert, Butcher's row
Marriott George (& woolstapler)
Cornhill
Preston & West, High st
Sills Elizth. & Frances, Sherrard st
Wall David (& Stilton cheesefactor)
Market place
MILLERS.
Hives Timothy, Nottingham road

To LEICESTER, the Alexander (from
Cambridge) calls at the George, every
Tuesday, Thursday and Saturday afternoon at four—the Champion (from Grantham) calls at the Fox, every Tuesday,
Thursday & Saturday morning at nine
—the Union (from Stamford) calls at the
Bell & Swan, every Wednesday, Friday
and Sunday evening at eight—a Van,
starts from the Stag & Pheasant, every
Wednesday and Saturday morning at
eight—and a Van (from Grantham) calls
at the Black Swan, every Monday,
Thursday and Saturday at one.
To NOTTINGHAM, a Van, from the Bell
and Swan, every Wednesday and Saturday morning at seven.
To STAMFORD, the Royal Mail (from
Birmingham) calls at the Fox, every afternoon at four; goes through Oakham
and the Union (from Leicester) calls at
the Bell & Swan, every Tuesday, Thursday and Saturday, at half-past one; goes
the same route.

CARRIERS.
To ASFORDBY, Michael Clarke, from the
White Lion, every Tuesday.
To BRAUNSTONE, George Lord, from
the Old Bishop Blaize, every Tuesday.
To BROUGHTON, John Taylor, from the
Fox, John Hensley, from the Bell and
Swan, and — Armstrong, from the Half
Moon, every Tuesday.
To BURROW, Thos. Mayfield, from the
Fox, every Tues. & Fri. & John Swing-
ler, from the Lord Nelson, every Tues.
To COSTON, Richard Dobney, from the
Old Bishop Blaize, every Tuesday.
To EATON, — Harris, from the Black
Moor's Head, every Tuesday.
To GREAT DALBY, James Prior, from
the Fleece, every Tuesday.
To GRANTHAM, Guido Dickinson, from
his house, High st. every Mon. and Fri.
To HARBY, Richd. Napp, from the White
Lion, every Tuesday.
To HICKLING, John Mann, from the
White Lion and Richard Topley, from
the Bell and Swan, every Tuesday.
To HOLWELL, Richd. Musson, from the
George and Dragon, every Tuesday.
To HOSE, Thos. Corner, from the Bull's
Head, every Tuesday.
To LANGHAM, Wm. Cox, from the Red
Lion, every Tuesday.
To LEICESTER, Guido Dickinson, from
his house, High st. every Saturday—

Pears Wm. Nottingham road
TAVERNS & PUBLIC HOUSES.
Black Moor's Head, Saml. Littler,
Market place [rard st
Black Swan, Joseph Oldham, Sher-
Boat, Ann Brewster, Burton end
Bricklayers' Arms, Joseph Waker-
ley, Timber hill [road
Bulls, Edw. Bawderson, Nottingham
Crown, Wm. Dickman, Burton end
Eight Bells, Hen. Measures, High st
Fox, Thomas Ward, Back st
Fox & Hounds, Mary Norfolk, High st
Generous Briton, Wm. Harrington
George & Dragon, Arthur Williams,
Burton end [st
Golden Fleece, John Marriott, Back
Half Moon, James Powell, Not-
tingham road [Burton end
Harborough Arms, Wm. Mason,
Lord Nelson, John Newby, Back st
Marquis of Granby, Thomas Free-
man, Sherrard st [end
Noel's Arms, Wm. Adcock, Burton
Old Bishop Blaize, Jos. Littlewood,
Sherrard st [st
Peacock, Henry Roberts, Sherrard
Red Lion, Wm. Oldham, Burton end
Rose & Crown, Wm Wakerley, King st
Stag & Pheasant, Wm. Cooke, High st
Three Crowns, Gideon Cooke,
Sherrard st [rard st
Wellington, Wm. Crossland, Sher-
Wheat Sheaf, Chas. Windows, Sher-
rard st [tingham road
White Lion, Timothy Hives, Not-
Woolpack, Wm. Smith, Sherrard st

Wm. Brown, from the Fleece, ever
Tuesday—Joseph Brewin, from the Stag
and Pheasant and Wm. Cox, from the
Red Lion, every Sat—Thos. Hext, from
the Stag & Pheasant, every Wed. & Sat.
—John Ashby, from the Fox, every Tues.
and Friday—and John Waite, from the
Black Swan, every Monday.
To LITTLE DALBY, John Clarke, from
the Red Lion, every Tuesday.
To LONG CLAWXTON, John Scar-
brough and — Wright, from the Half
Moon, every Tuesday.
To LOUGHBOROUGH, — Fewkes, from
the Crown, and — Ecclesfield, from the
Noel's Arms, every Tuesday—Joseph
Brewin, from the Stag & Pheasant, and
John Beadsby, from the Red Lion,
every Thursday.
To NEWARK, Guido Dickinson, from his
house, High st, every Wednesday.
To NOTTINGHAM, John Taylor, from
the Fox, every Wednesday.
To OAKHAM, John Barsby, from the
Fox, & Thomas Canner, from the Red
Lion, every Tuesday.
To OLD DALBY, — Halliwell, from the
Half Moon, every Tuesday.
To REARSBY, Rebecca Thompson, from
the Crown, every Tuesday.
To SEAGRAVE, Will am Chester, from
the Fox, every Tuesday.
To SEALFORD, Richard Glover, from
the White Lion, every Tuesday.
To SOMERBY, William Tebbs, from the
Crown and William Dauzey, from the
George & Dragon, every Tuesday.
To SPROXTON, John Stanley, from the
Black Swan, every Tuesday.
To STONESBY, — Hutchinson, from the
George & Dragon, every Tuesday.
To SYSTON, Sarah Soutar, from the
Fox, John Cooper, from the Black Moor's
Head, and Edwd. Parker, from the Pea-
cock, every Tuesday.
To THRUSSINGTON, Joseph Brewin,
from the Stag & Pheasant, every Tues.
To TWYFORD, Thomas Ward, from the
Fox, every Tuesday.
To UPPINGHAM, John Barsby, from the
Fox, every Wednesday.
To WALTON, John Osborne, from the
Peacock, every Tuesday.
To WHISSINDINE, John Green & John
Burbank, from the Red Lion, every Tues.
To WYMONDHAM, Ann Rimington,
from the Fox & Jervis James, from the
Crown, every Tuesday.

The population of the town grew throughout the 1800's, from 1766 inhabitants in 1801, to 3327 in 1831, 3740 in 1851 and 5033 in 1871 . However, the 1871 figure is recorded as *including a number of persons visiting the steeplechases, and 126 paupers in the workhouse'* so how reliable the figure are is open to doubt. They do give an indication of a growing town, though.

THE WORKHOUSE

This was first recorded in 1777 when an establishment existed with accommodation for up to forty inmates, but the location is uncertain. In 1835 there was a workhouse on back Street.

A new workhouse was erected in 1836 on Thorpe Road at a cost of £6000, to the design of Charles Dyer, using an elongated H plan. It didn't just cater for Melton town but the wider area around it, the population it covered totalling 17,872 in 1831. By 1835 the average poor rate expenditure per year was £9433, or 10s 7d per head of population.

A vagrants block was built south of the workhouse with work cells for stone breaking.

In 1869-70 a new infirmary was built next to the workhouse which has become the town hospital with many of the original buildings still in place.

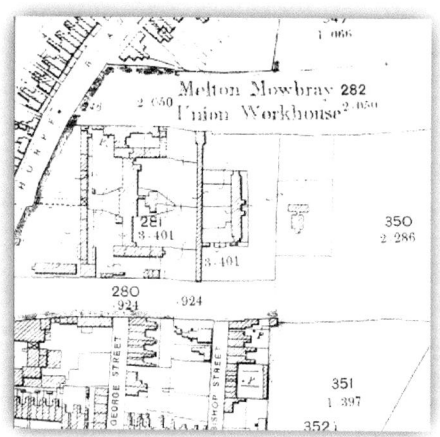

A plan of the workhouse showing he distinctive H shaped plan.

Staff in 1846 comprised the Master and Mistress, Joseph and Jane Bell, and a Chaplain, Rev. G Oakley.

There were four staff in 1881, a Master and Matron, Samuel and Martha Weston and Joseph and Annie Thompson, the school master and mistress. Both were married couples and looked after 160 inmates of whom 48 were listed as 'scholars'. This indicates that the workhouse was looking after orphaned children as well as adult inmates and that they were educated on the premises rather than being sent out to school.

Four staff were sufficient because all the chores would be done by the inmates.

The original workhouse buildings in use in March 2015 as part of St Mary's Hospital.

The hospital buildings built in 1870 behind the workhouse; the flat roofed section is more recent.

The well known picture of Burton End in the 19th century, showing the stone arched bridge spanning the River Eye with the old ford to the right of it. Beyond that is the Railway Hotel, as far as I know the only time it appears in a photograph before being demolished in 1900. There is a low bridge to allow the road over the ford to pass beneath the railway, and to the left of that is the level crossing and signal box. The ford could be used rather than wait for the crossing to open if the river was fairly low. The church tower can just be glimpsed in the distance; I wish I had a better copy of the picture but sadly I haven't. The date is uncertain but it is post 1870 as the signal box was not installed until then.

Thorpe End looking from Sherrard Street in about 1890, with the White Hart on the right.

THE JUBILEE FOUNTAIN.

This facility was erected to mark the Jubilee of Queen Victoria in 1887, initially in the marketplace. Made of cast iron and topped with a lantern it cost the town £26 17s 10d and was designed by George Smith of Glasgow. It was supplied as a kit of parts and was erected by local builder C. Barnes, plumbed in by John Anderson, and then the Melton Gas Light Company connected up the lantern. It wasn't a decorative fountain but a drinking fountain, and became something of a gathering point for groups of youths.

Sadly the fountain was not popular in the town and the local tradesmen petitioned to have it removed. It was re-erected in Play Close, but was scrapped in 1940 when all metal items were being collected for the war effort.

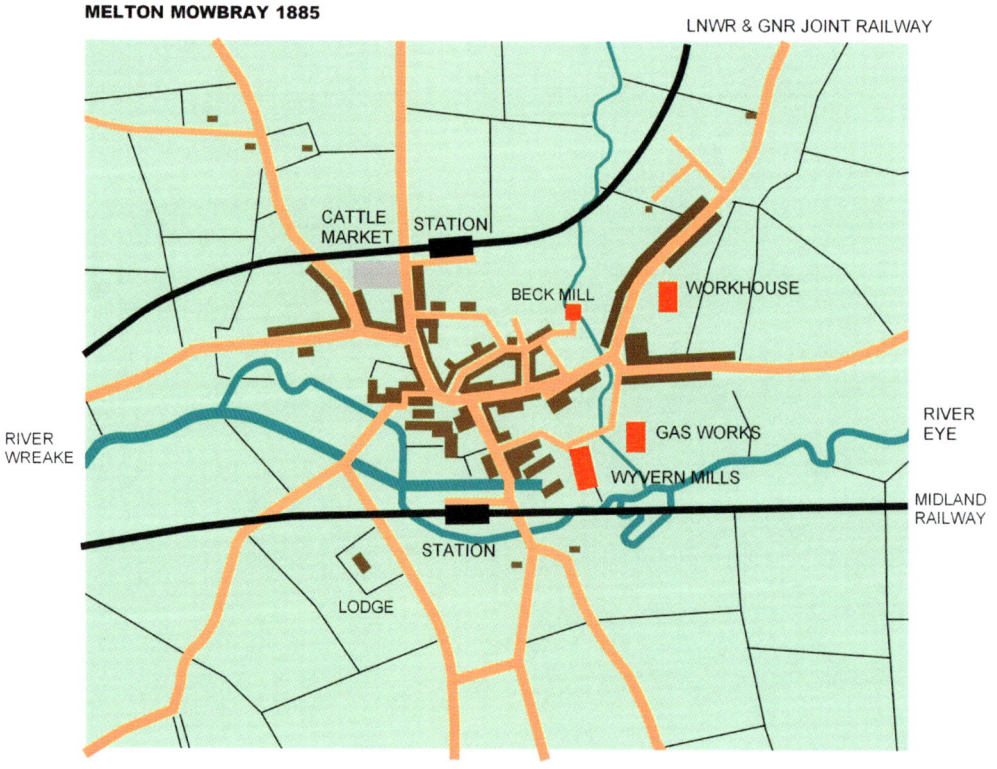

MELTON MOWBRAY 1885

LNWR & GNR JOINT RAILWAY

CATTLE MARKET

STATION

BECK MILL

WORKHOUSE

RIVER WREAKE

GAS WORKS

WYVERN MILLS

RIVER EYE

MIDLAND RAILWAY

STATION

LODGE

ASFORDBY RD

NORMAN ST

PALL MALL

BENTLEY ST

CHAPEL ST

BACK PARK

NOTTINGHAM ST

WILTON ST

SAGE CROSS ST

GEORGE HOTEL

BELL HOTEL

KING ST

RUTLAND ST

THORPE END

HIGH ST

SHERRARD ST

LEICESTER ST

MARKET PLACE

RIVER WREAKE

LEICESTER RD

BURTON ST

MILL ST

THE TOWN CENTRE IN 1885

HARBOROUGH HOTEL

1. St MARY'S CHURCH 2. EGERTON PARK
3. MAGISTRATES COURT 4. THE LIMES 5. BECK MILL

The 1877 Trade Directory gives a fascinating insight into how many different occupations were being carried out in the town at that time, most of them small concerns as there were few large firms in Melton then.

Excluding all the publicans, brewers etc. as they are covered in a later chapter, this is a snapshot of life in Melton:

SHOPS etc: greengrocer, tailor & draper, grocer, ale & porter merchant, chemist & druggist, baker, butcher, pork pie manufacturer, confectioner, furniture broker, hosier & haberdasher, milliner, cheese makers, hatter & hosier, fishmonger, toy seller, tobacconist, picture framer, dressmaker, sewing machine dealer, wine merchant, piano and harmonium dealer, glass and china dealer, straw bonnet maker, pharmacist, banker, hairdresser, bookseller, outfitter.

TRADES Plumber and Glazier, bootmaker, paperhanger & painter, grazier, builder & contractor, brick maker, chimney sweep, rope, twine and wagon cover manufacturer, leather dealers, cutlery manufacturers, dentist, doctor, eating house proprietor and plasterer, bricklayer, head groom, foreman, coal dealer, carrier, cattle dealer, whitesmith and gas fitter, fellmonger, brick, tile and sanitary ware manufacturer, farmer, iron and brass founders, basketmaker, brush manufacturer, timber merchant, tobacco pipe manufacturer, wheelwright, trap builder (horse drawn vehicle), nail manufacturer, coachbuilder, nurseryman and seed dealer, ironmonger, cabinetmaker and joiner, well sinker, blacksmith, soda water manufacturer, saddle and harness maker, tinplate worker, clock maker, horse dealer, gardener, corn merchant, agricultural implement makers, cooper, dog biscuit manufacturer, organ builder, miller, watch maker, tanner, stone mason, basket maker.

PROFESSIONS Accountant, teacher, valet, Vicar, auctioneer, solicitor and solicitor's clerk, lawyer, highway and nuisance inspector & surveyor, medical assistant, professor of music and drawing, school mistress, veterinary inspector, police inspector, music teacher, Gas works manager, rector, insurance broker, railway inspector, architect, watchmaker & jeweller, registrar, engineer, printer & bookbinder, librarian, postmaster, bailiff, missionary, stamp distributer, workhouse master and matron, photographer, station master, naturalist, undertaker, commercial traveller, surgeon, gunsmith.

Melton was a very self contained town, with nearly everything produced on the doorstep as was the way in the nineteenth century. There were few large employers other than perhaps the railways; the likes of the Wyvern Mills were still in the future.

A tranquil scene on Burton Street in about 1890 with the Almshouses on the right. This is one of the few scenes in the book that looks very similar today. The town was gas lit then; a lamp can be seen on the right.

This is Ankle Hill, or what we now know as Warwick Road, looking down the hill towards Burton Road before there had been any building or development.

THE CARRIERS

In all towns in the 19th century the carriers cart was a common sight; even after the advent of the railway they were an essential part of the local economy, connecting the villages to Melton, especially those without a station. Not until motorised transport became affordable after 1918 did they die out, replaced by lorries which were often war surplus sold off very cheaply. The horse drawn carriers cart was a centuries old tradition, and each village was served by its own carrier who was based in Melton at a particular inn. This meant that people knew where to find them, a bit like a bus stop or taxi rank today.

Many of the carriers only operated on Tuesdays, market day, there being no demand for their services on other days when a trip to town was at most a weekly treat. They carried produce and passengers if there was still room, anything that needed to be transported.

These are the carriers serving Melton in 1877, operating only on Tuesday unless noted:

ASFORDBY Waterson from the Eight Bells.

ASHBY FOLVILLE & BARSBY Swift from the Noels Arms.

BARROW Levesland from the Granby.

BRANSTON Ryder from the Bishop Blaize.

BROOKSBY Ward from the Fox.

THE BROUGHTONS Pick & Cooper from the Half Moon.

BUCKMINSTER Bartram fro the Peacock.

BURROUGH Mayfield from the Noels Arms, *also Fridays*.

CLAWSON Paget & Robinson, from the White Lion.

COSTON Rose from the Bishop Blaize.

CROXTON Farnsworth from the Granby.

GREAT DALBY Woolley from the Fox.

LITTLE DALBY Wheat from the Crown.

OLD DALBY Woodford from the White Lion.

EASTWELL & EATON Harrison from the Half Moon and Hubbard from the King's Head.

EDMONTHORPE Sleath from the Granby.

FRISBY Hornbuckle from the Black's Head & Marriott from the Golden Fleece.

GADDESBY Walker from the Fox.

GARTHORPE Rose from the Bishop Blaize.

GOADBY MARWOOD Harrison from the Half Moon & Hubbard from the King's Head.

GRIMSTON Woodford from the White Lion.

HARBY Starbuck from the White Lion & Kemp from the Half Moon.

HOBY Ward from the Fox.

HOSE Stubbs from the Jolly Butcher.

KETTLEBY Martin from the King's Head.

KNOSSINGTON Tidd from the Crown.

LEICESTER Bramley from the Crown.

MARKET OVERTON Faulks from the Half Moon & Leverland from the Granby.

OWSTON Tidd from the Crown.

PICKWELL Wheal and Tidd from the Crown.

PLUNGAR Morris from the White Lion.

REARSBY Bramley from the Crown.

ROTHERBY Ward from the Fox.

SALTBY Rode from the Bishop Blaize.

SAXBY Rose from the Bishop Blaize.

SAXELBY Woodford from the White Lion.

SOMERBY Wheat from the Crown.

SPROXTON Pick from the Black Sawn & Everitt from the Black's head.

STATHERN Poyser from the White Lion, Alderman & Woodcock from the Black's Head.

STONESBY Brewster from the Black Swan.

SYSTON Bramley from the Crown.

TEIGH Faulks from the Half Moon.

THORPE SATCHVILLE Walker from the Fox.

THRUSSINGTON Eyre from the Fox.

TWYFORD Walker from the Fox.

WALTHAM Brewster from the Black Swan & Hubbard from the King's Head.

WHISSENDINE Stafford from the Noels Arms & Walker from the Crown.

WYMESWOLD Smith from the Fox.

WYMONDHAM F. Shield from the Crown, *(also Thursday and Saturday),* W. Shield from the Black's Head and Hickman from the Bishop Blaize.

It seems strange to see a cart serving Leicester, thirty years after the railway had opened, but of course the cart also served the villages en-route and the station could be a long way from the village centre, not to mention being more expensive.

Several of the Inns were the base for more than one cart while others had none; maybe a large yard was necessary as the cart would have to be parked during the day and the horses fed and watered. Tuesdays must have been a bustling scene, especially before the market was moved to Scalford Road....in fact it must have been bedlam!

These pictures are not of Melton carriers but they do give an impression of what these carts looked like in the second half of the nineteenth century.

THE COLLES HALL

Colles Hall on Burton Street is now occupied by a Pizza Express. Dr Colles was first the curate and then vicar of St Mary's Church. The hall replaced the George and Dragon Inn which Dr Colles lived next to. As President of the Melton Temperance Society, Dr Colles did not approve of drinking and when the landlord passed away he bought the Inn in order to close it down and built this rather fanciful private house on the site.

THE CORN EXCHANGE

Built in Nottingham Street during 1854, for the first time the trading of grain was brought under one roof rather than taking place in the open. It opened on 1st August 1855 and trading took place there until the building was converted into an entrance for the Bell Centre in about 1980. Construction was funded by local businessmen, and two surgeons paid for the bell in the handsome clock tower. The building also contained at various times the Magistrates Court, a bank, a library and the County Court.

Although it looks from the front like a complete building sadly as with the Bell Hotel only the front façade remains of the original structure.

Leicester Road looking towards the town in the 1890's with fields on either side; these would later be developed into the town parks.

Nottingham Street about the turn of the century; the street surface is granite setts. The Eight Bells pub is on the right.

THE MELTON TIMES

Melton's newspaper, the Melton Times, originated in the nineteenth century. The first edition was published on August 16th 1859 but it came from Westgate in Grantham as it was meant as a companion paper to the existing Grantham Times.

The cost for the first issue was a penny, and the front page was pretty much filled with advertisements from local businesses; the news came inside the paper. Sadly the venture was not a success and after only fifteen months the paper ceased to be produced……it did better than an earlier paper, the Melton Recorder, which began in the 1840's and only lasted for ten months!

This wasn't the end of the Melton Times though as the title was used again in 1887 for a new paper, this time published in the town. On March 19th the first edition of what was really the Melton Times appeared, printed and published from premises at 1, Chapel Street in Melton. The owner was Henry Towell, and James Morley and Nat Brown were also directors of the company. The building was just a small cottage, where Chapel Street met King Street and the printing was done in the cellar, the presses operated by a one armed man. Apparently half the cogs were missing from the machinery and the noise had to be heard to be believed!

Fortunately a new building had been procured in Nottingham Street which is where the paper is still based to this day.

THE MELTON MOWBRAY BUILDING SOCIETY

The Melton Mowbray building society is another nineteenth century company, having been established in 1875 and is one of the oldest surviving building societies in the United Kingdom with over 65,000 members. It provides mortgages, savings, insurance and investment products from its principal office and three branches in Melton Mowbray, Oakham and Grantham.

The Melton is a mutual organisation owned by its members. An impressive new headquarters was built on Leicester Road in the early 2000's.

WHAT REMAINS TO BE SEEN?

Victorian Melton can still be glimpsed if you know where to look.

Kings Road, now cut short by Norman Way. The houses on this section are nineteenth century and make perfectly good homes in 2015; what a shame so many streets like this were swept away.

Beck Mill; the medieval corn mill was redundant by the mid 1800's so it was demolished and in its place this cloth mill was built. The old mill pond was filled in, and even the brook that drove the mill wheel can no longer be seen.

Typical Victorian house backs; the fronts face Thorpe Road.

Shoulers saleroom on Kings Road, a former school building built in the late 1800's; despite all the alterations that have been made it still has the little cupola with the bell inside.

CHAPTER 7

ST MARY'S CHURCH

Melton Church is a fine building and dominates the skyline from all approaches to the town; it must have done so even more in Medieval times.

The Church was originally always called 'St Mary the Virgin' , the name possibly being altered during the Dissolution. This is not the first Church to have stood on the site as in Saxon times a building of some sort would certainly have been in use, but no record of it has survived. It is possible that part of an earlier building was reused in the lower part of the tower around the staircase when that was constructed in the mid 12th century.

The earliest written record concerning the Church relates to a gift from Robert de Mowbray in 1170 for the building of the lower part of the staircase, nicely dating the first phase of construction. Work continued in phases until the last recorded gift in 1532. Buildings such as this were never finished in one go, it was simply too big a project, though the main structure would have been recognisable by about 1300. The last work was the completion of the tower and the clerestory.

The architectural styles change along with the period of construction. The early parts are in Early English, then the later work is Perpendicular.

Both brown and grey stone were used, sourced locally probably from Somerby and Clipsham. It would all have had to be brought in by cart, a laborious process even over those short distances.

The vestry of the Church was the last addition and it has the date, 1532, carved into the stonework. Some of the stones used in the building are said to have come from the then derelict hospital at Burton Lazars, a sensible recycling of easily available materials if true but it is difficult to prove either way.

The Church has a peal of ten bells; the first reference is writing dates from 1546 when the 'clock and chimes' were mentioned but they no doubt existed long before that. There were six bells in 1552 and there are numerous references to work being done on them. The six bells sufficed until 1802 when two more were added, the final two being hung in 1894. They were removed during World war Two and left lying in the churchyard so when they were rehung in 1946 the chance was taken to recast some of them. All the oldest bells have been recast over the years.

The Carillion that plays the chimes was renewed in 1938 as was the clock, which had been in place since just before the battle of Trafalgar.

INTERIOR MELTON MOWBRAY PARISH CHURCH.

During the Civil War Roundhead troops were billeted in the Church and the Coat of Arms above the arch was used for target practice; the holes made by the musket balls can still be seen.

The area close to the Church is a delight, possibly the most un-spoiled area in the town. Church Street is an ancient thorough-fare, shown on the map from 1500 and certainly dating back long before then.

The narrowness of the street is typically Medieval, when the largest thing that had to pass along it was a horse. Before Burton Street existed this was the main road from London! Thankfully later de-velopments allowed traffic to bypass this area, leaving it unchanged.

This is a glimpse of ancient Melton, alt-hough the brick buildings are eighteenth century at the oldest.

Running parallel to Church Street is Park Lane, which is just as old and also full of character.

OTHER PLACES OF WORSHIP IN MELTON

The parish church has naturally always been the focal point for religious observance, but there were other places of worship in the town too.

The first nonconformist chapel was built following the raising of funds begun in 1818, services previously having been held at the Playhouse in High Street which may not have been conducive to thinking about higher things! The chapel opened in 1821, and the building remains today.

The first Methodist chapel was built in 1796, the members of the Melton Society numbering only eleven it did not need to be very large. It was enlarged in 1725 by which time membership had risen to three figures, and a new building was erected on the same site in 1871.

Primitive Methodists were a distinct group and had their own chapel on Goodriche Street, built in 1845. In 1888 a church was built on Sherrard Street, but it was demolished in 1973.

The Roman Catholic church was built in 1842 to a design by Pugin; since then two further Catholic churches have been built further out of town.

The Chapel alongside Norman Way, originally Norman Street; I believe this is the chapel erected in 1818, and it is now used for a nursery school.

CHAPTER 8

THE MELTON MOWBRAY NAVIGATION

AND THE OAKHAM CANAL

In the eighteenth century transporting goods meant using a lumbering cart, often drawn by oxen, or pack animals such as horses or mules. This was just about acceptable for high value low bulk items such as Stilton cheese, but when it came to moving coal it was very different matter. As the town grew in size a source of reasonably priced coal became ever more desirable, but the nearest coalfields were the far side of Leicester, in Nottinghamshire and Derbyshire. Transport costs were horrific; the mines might as well have been on the moon for all the real use they were to the people of Melton.

Canals had already begun to be built in the East Midlands, and naturally attracted the attention of local businessmen. The Soar had been made navigable as early as 1778 as far as Loughborough, connecting with the Trent nine miles away. By 1790 all the main coal producing areas were connected by canal, but none of this helped the situation in Melton. It would take local initiative to resolve the situation.

The first proposals for making the River Wreake navigable were made in 1780 but these came to nothing; the scheme was revived in 1785 and with much local support including crucially The Earl of Harborough of Stapleford Hall a survey was commissioned from William Jessop. The first meeting was held at the Swan Inn in Melton market place on November 16th and £6000 was subscribed. The only voices raised in opposition were the mine owners of Leicestershire who saw their high prices would be challenged if coal could be brought in from other coalfields.

In January 1786 it was resolved to apply to Parliament, the proposal being split into two halves. The first was to make the Soar navigable from Loughborough to Leicester and the second was for the Wreake to Melton. The bill was read in April but was defeated, influenced by powerful interests in Leicester. Obviously the second part was of no value if the Soar could not be made navigable first. A revised bill was presented, combining the two parts, but it was again defeated in May 1789. The plan was too important to be forgotten though, and finally the Leicester Navigation Act received Royal Assent on 13th May 1791.

The work began promptly but construction was delayed by lack of skilled labour and rising costs due to inflation caused by the Napoleonic wars, and it was not until a second Act had been passed extending the time allowed for construction that the canal opened through to Melton during 1797. There was no ceremony, in fact the opening passed pretty much unrecorded.

The canal was fourteen and a half miles long, and terminated in a basin at Melton alongside Burton Street between Burton End bridge and the town centre. The route separated from the river at the edge of the town and an independent channel was dug, part of which can still be seen close to the swimming pool.

Almost as soon as the canal had opened the idea of extending it to Oakham had been mooted, and the basin at Melton was laid out with this in mind.

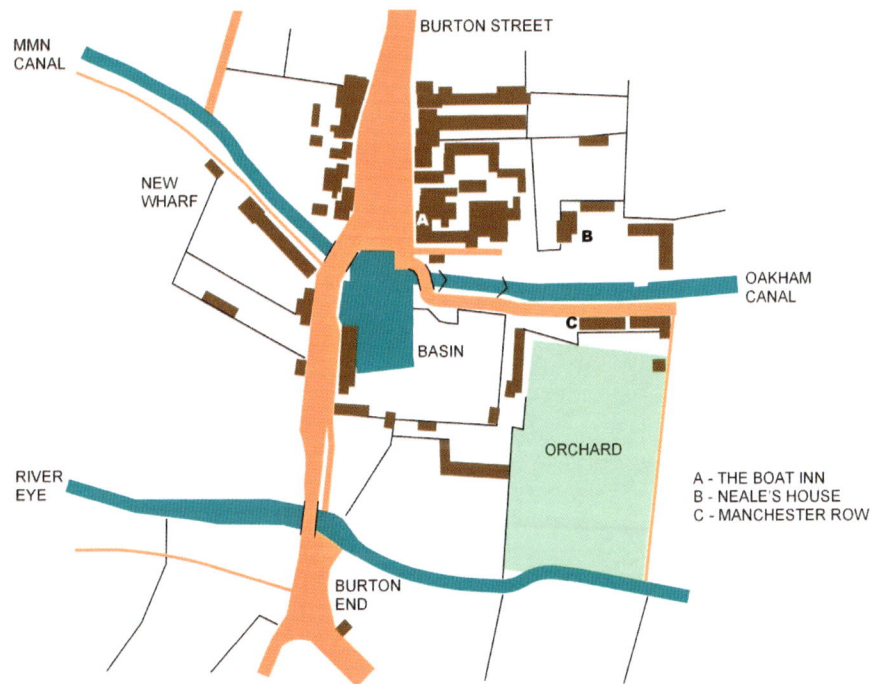

The Melton Mowbray Navigation approached from the west while the river ran further south in a wide loop around the town. Burton Road passed over an arched stone bridge alongside which was a ford which was probably the original crossing point.

The Oakham canal act was passed in 1793, very soon after the canal to Melton opened, so it was clearly well on the cards while the Wreake work was being carried out and it was a logical next move; in fact the original intention was to go all the way to Stamford. Again however raising money was difficult and a second act was needed before the Oakham canal could be opened. This took place in June 1802 although it was not useable through to Oakham until the following year.

The arrangement at Melton was that the basin connected the two canals, the Oakham canal requiring a lock to reach the right level. A brick bridge took Burton Street over the MMN canal, and a low brick wall edged the basin to the north with a grass bank above it topped by a fence. Another brick bridge spanned the entrance to the Oakham canal, giving access to the wharf along which warehouses and other buildings were constructed. The southern side of the basin was not walled, the water lapping against the open ground. The wharf was where boats unloaded, the basin was purely for turning. To the north of the canal buildings were soon added on land owned by Joseph Neale including the Boat Inn, now the last remnant of the enterprise. To the south of the canal was a long terrace of workers houses called Birmingham Row which was not demolished until about 1970. There was also a house for the toll keeper John Willis adjacent to the lock.

A wharf was built on the south side of the NNM canal to the west of the bridge alongside which a warehouse was built with other smaller buildings. One building was later incorporated into the station goods yard when the area was redeveloped in 1846 and survived until about 1960.

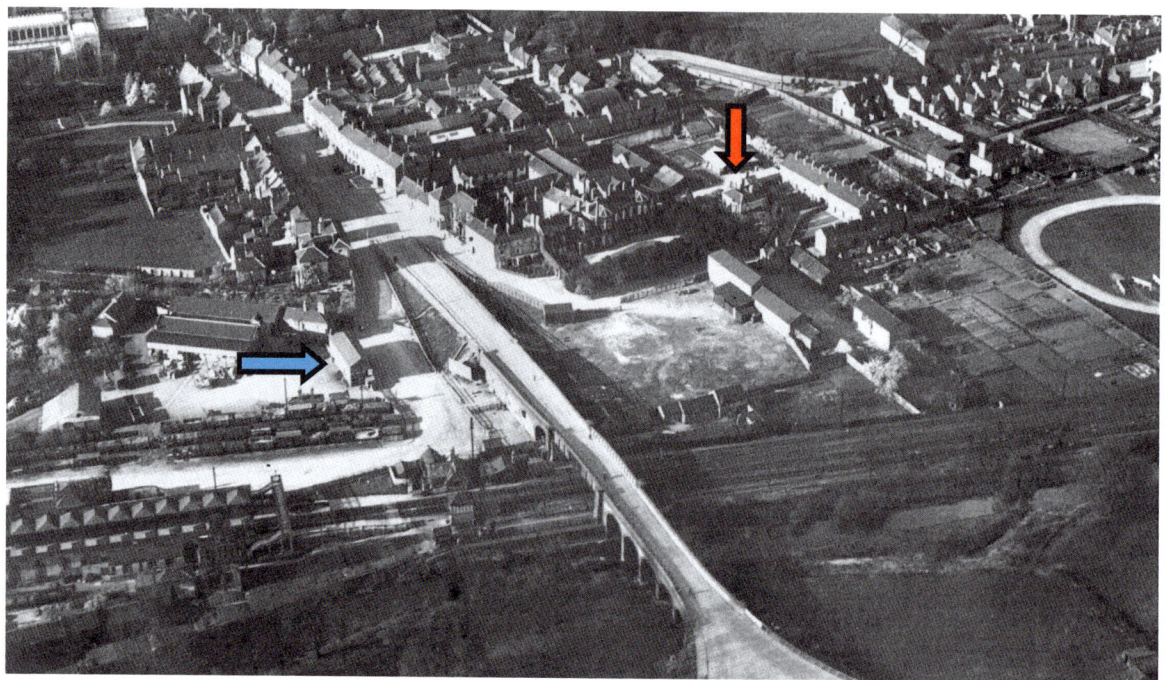

Photo courtesy of English Heritage.

Burton End in 1926 showing the site of the canal basin which had been filled in but not developed at that point. Many of the canal buildings were still in place including the warehouse formerly serving the new wharf, marked by the blue arrow on the photo. Towards the right a terrace of houses crosses the course of the Oakham canal, south of which is Birmingham row which stood alongside it.

The canal basin in about 1870, looking along Burton Street towards the town. The barge is alongside the brick wall, and the road bridges are seen to the left and right, that on the left carrying Burton Street. The Boat Inn is on the right with the sign hanging from the front wall. The main road now runs straight through the middle of this scene.

The canals provided a useful service to the community from the first part of the nineteenth century; if not exactly prospering they were at least solvent. Half the coal carried by the MMN continued along the Oakham canal. Between 1839 and 1842 the wharves at Melton dealt with 6287 tons of merchandise, but that was the end of the prosperous years as a new form of transport threatened to take away the traffic from both canals. In the early 1840's railways were the coming thing and canals were suddenly under threat, seen as slow and old fashioned.

The Oakham canal reduced its tolls but when a railway between Syston and Peterborough was proposed by George Husdon the canal was unable to compete, and even worse it was right in the way of the proposed route. The Midland Railway bought the canal, closed it and for much of its length filled it in and built the new railway on top.

The MMN canal was pretty much unaffected physically, but trade wise it was a disaster. It struggled on with traffic reducing year on year, dropping from 53640 tons in 1845, the year before the railway opened, to only 17087 in 1851. Final closure came on 1st August 1877.

In Melton when the Oakham canal closed the basin remained in use, but the lock was removed and the old Oakham canal filled in. The new station goods yard used the site of the New Wharf but the MMN canal remained, running north of the goods yard on its original course. Happily this meant that the canal was still there as photography became popular so that the scene was recorded for posterity.

After closure the basin remained in place until 1883 when it was filled in but the site was not developed for many years; similarly the course of the canal itself could be traced as the old towpath became a narrow road running along the north edge of the station goods yard.

Part of the canal retains water close to the Leisure Centre, and the Boat Inn continues to thrive, giving a link to this chapter in the history of the town.

The house built for Joseph Neale north of the canal in 1837. It is marked by the red arrow in the photo on the previous page. Neal was the surveyor of the canal. All the buildings in this area were demolished in the early 1970's to allow for the enlargement of the Pedigree factory.

The bridge crossing the entrance to the Oakham canal from the basin, looking west towards the basin with the lock behind the photographer.

What remains to be seen?

The Boat Inn is the most tangible reminder of the canal, with the road in front the former route to the Oakham canal wharf.

Around the corner from the Boat these attractive houses all date from around the building of the canal in 1790 –1800, and happily survived the enlargement of the Pedigree factory in the 1970's.

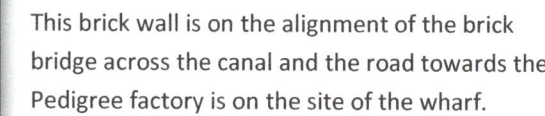

This brick wall is on the alignment of the brick bridge across the canal and the road towards the Pedigree factory is on the site of the wharf.

The stone gateposts would have been in situ when the canal was in use, the road running along the north bank serving the houses. The commercial activity took place on the south side of the canal, but it would still have been a busy, bustling place unlike the tranquil scene today.

Looking back from the route of the canal towards the Boat Inn; the canal ran to the right of the buildings with the basin to the right off the picture.

In the foreground is the carpark for the council offices.

The route of the canal is marked across the park by this avenue of trees, mature now but perhaps planted when the canal was built to shade the towpath. This view is looking west away from the basin.

At the end of the path a pair of lock gates are embedded in the ground to mark the site of the canal. This view is looking east towards the basin and the wharves. In fact there was no lock here so they have been brought from elsewhere.

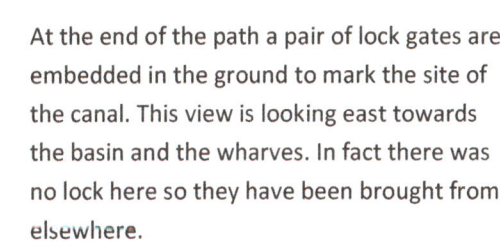

The peaceful scene from the footbridge across the river outside the swimming pool, looking along the length of canal towards Leicester Road. This gives a good indication of how the canal must have looked when it was in use. The River Eye runs left to right alongside the park towards Lady Wilton bridge. The footbridge crosses the river rather than the canal, so it is probably original.

CHAPTER 9

THE RAILWAYS

The opening of the canals transformed life in Melton but their period of dominance would last for less than fifty years, and their downfall was dramatic and irreversible.

The advent of railways in the 1830's lead to an explosion of schemes across the country, and in many cases it was the movement of goods that was important rather than people. London in particular had a huge appetite for coal , and the railway company that could gain a foothold moving that coal form the Midlands would make a fortune. In the 1830's it was mainly shipped from the North East, but that was expensive and could easily be undercut by a railway. George Hudson of York, the unscrupulous 'Railway King', had his eye on the prize. He had opened the Midland Counties Railway from Derby to Leicester in May 1840 and the Eastern Counties from Peterborough to London was due to open in 1847; now he needed to join the two together. That's how Melton Mowbray, almost incidentally, came to be on the railway map.

Hudson planned a route leaving he Midland Counties line north of Leicester at Syston, running east to Melton, then via Oakham and Stamford to Peterborough. It would very conveniently serve three important towns en-route, but that wasn't the reason for building the line….it was to move coal to London. It was a very round-about route, but speed didn't matter, and it was not until later that more direct routes were built including that south from Leicester to St Pancras. Once the coal could go that way the Syston and Peterborough settled down to a quiet existence.

The line was promoted as an independent company but it was always intended that it would be a part of the Midland Railway which Hudson was developing by absorbing smaller companies such as the Midland Counties. By the time the S&P had opened there was no longer any pretence and it was thought of as a branch of the Midland Railway.

The line reached Melton Mowbray from Syston, but to begin with it terminated at a temporary wooden station close to the Dalby Road bridge. This was because Hudson was having trouble with the Earl of Harborough who didn't like the idea of the new railway crossing his park at Stapleford. It didn't help when a tunnel being dug to hide the line collapsed! The Earl had holdings in the Oakham canal company which didn't make him view the railway with any enthusiasm. The line opened as far as Melton on 1st September 1846 but it was not until 1st May 1848 that it could continue to Oakham and beyond. The power of landowners in those days was formidable!

In the meantime work began on erecting the new station to serve Melton Mowbray; the New Wharf on the MMN canal was filled in and the station site was levelled between the canal and the River Eye. There was some opposition in the town, but work progressed quickly so that it would be ready when the line could be opened throughout.

MELTON MOWBRAY MIDLAND STATION 1885

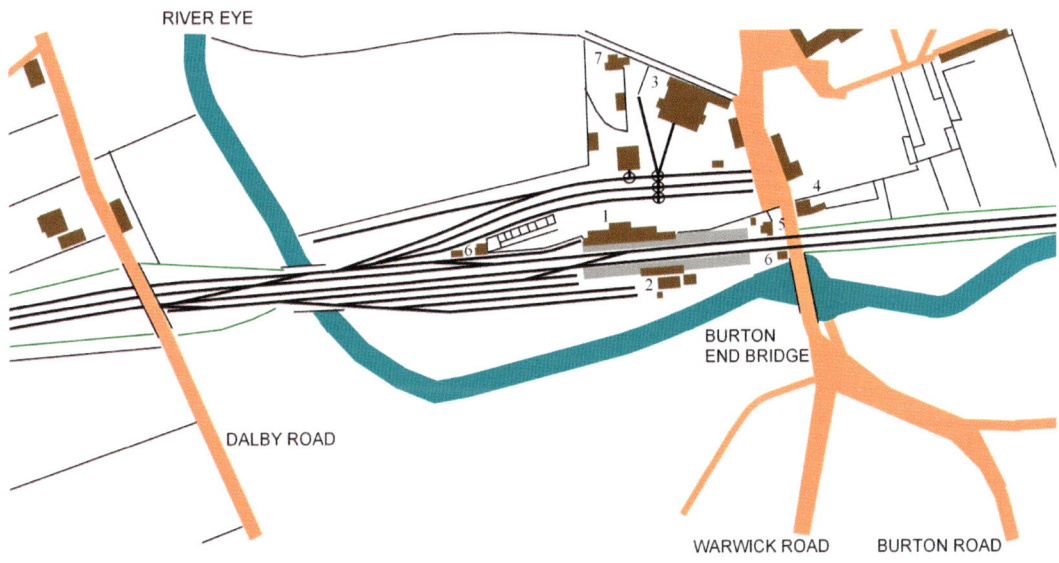

1 - STATION BUILDING 2 - SHELTER AND WATER TOWER 3 - GOODS SHED 4 - RAILWAY HOTEL
5 - LEVEL CROSSING COTTAGE 6 - SIGNAL BOX 7 - STATION MASTERS HOUSE

The new station opened to passengers on 1st May 1848 but freight had already begun to use the facilities in March 20th. The site was quite confined, with the river to the south and the narrow bridge carrying Dalby Road to the west. Much of the goods yard was laid out on the filled in canal wharf, and the arrangement here reflected the early date of the construction. Railways in 1848 were still a new technology, feeling their way with little accepted practice to fall back on.

The goods yard was laid out with three long sidings, but the goods shed was separate and could only be accessed using wagon turntables. This meant that unloading wagons under cover was a laborious business; shunting would have used horses, and a small stable was provided nearby. In the early days it wasn't a great problem, but as time went on it proved impossible for railways to introduce larger more efficient wagons because the wheelbase was constrained by yards such as Melton. Not until the late 1950's was something finally done to improve the situation, a new goods shed being built alongside the further siding; unfortunately by that time small stations such as Melton had little freight traffic left to be handled.

The other odd thing about the new Midland station was the quality of the architecture. On the same line, Oakham and Stamford had charming station buildings built to the highest standards and designed by noted architects; no expense was spared. At Melton, though, haunt of the aristocracy and even Royalty, a plain red brick edifice was erected that had no architectural merit whatsoever! There was an overall roof to keep the weather off, but other than that it was functional, to put it politely.

The overall roof collapsed under the weight of snow in 1861, so it can't have been particularly well built!

There were two platforms; the only traffic was through trains, no services began or ended here so that was ample provision. Burton Road crossed the line by means of a level crossing just before Burton End Bridge and a cottage was erected for the crossing keeper. The red brick Railway Hotel was built on the opposite side of Burton Road by the crossing, this surviving until the road bridge was built in 1900. Beyond the crossing the double tracked line ran east towards Saxby.

This is a view of the station in 1926, not looking very different from when it opened other than for the provision of the ridge and furrow awnings in 1879....there seems to be no record of what kept the weather off the passengers between then and the overall roof collapsing. The goods yard is full to bursting, emphasising the difficulty of getting wagons in and out of the goods shed....a lot would have been loaded in the open. The lime-washed cattle pens can be seen towards the left, and in the foreground the buildings were used for repairing wagons. On the extreme right can be seem the water tank standing behind the Leicester platform. A lot of coaches are standing in the sidings , either stored or having been used for a special working. What cannot be seen from this angle is the arched portico erected in 1879 at the same time as the canopies in order to make the station look more impressive in view of the Joint station that had just opened across town....it didn't work!

The station received proper signalling for the first time in 1877 when two signal boxes were erected, one by the level crossing and Melton Sidings box at the entrance to the goods yard. Life went on in much the same way day by day, until suddenly Melton station found itself on the main line from London to Scotland!

The problem for the Midland Railway was at Leicester; there simply weren't enough tracks for the traffic using the line and it was causing a bottle neck. The solution was to build a new line across the Welland valley from Kettering to Manton on the Syston and Peterborough line, so that the express trains to the north could use this route and bypass Leicester. They would then run up through Oakham and Melton, running onto another new line just to the west of Melton which took them off the S&P and straight to Nottingham. So it was that much of the Anglo-Scottish traffic from St Pancras could be seen running through Melton station; not that it made any difference to the townspeople, of course, because none of the trains stopped!

One thing leads to another; now the Oakham to Melton section became clogged with traffic so long loop lines were laid east of Melton station as far as Brentingby Junction which enabled passenger trains to overtake the slower freights. The loops opened in 1904 and the chance was taken to install water troughs at the same time.

With the increase in trains using the line the level crossing at Melton as becoming a problem, even with the light levels of road traffic at the time. The decision was made to replace it with a bridge, not easy on the constricted site. The Railway Hotel was closed and demolished, and a long brick bridge was erected with a metal span crossing the tracks. The new bridge opened in 1900 and the level crossing was closed; at the same time the old stone bridge over the river was demolished. The new arrangement wasn't pretty, but image the chaos now if it hadn't been built!

This is Burton End in 1926, showing the new bridge clearly. Little else had changed, the crossing cottage and signal box can still be seen and the station approach road is the former road heading for the level crossing...a footbridge has been provided, though, erected in 1897. The junction between Burton Road and Warwick Road was now at a much higher level; there was little building at this time south of the river, though this would change dramatically.

Traffic had built up through Melton in part because a new line had opened to Saxby in 1892, the Midland and Great Northern Joint line which ran all the way to Great Yarmouth, though not very quickly. The bright yellow engines from the M&GN could be seen at Melton because they ran through to Leicester and Nottingham and these trains stopped as well, opening up new possibilities for Summer holidays.

Little more changed at Melton station until 1942, when the two Midland signal boxes were removed and a single box was built to replace them, the one that still controls the station today.

As already mentioned, the goods yard was finally reorganised in the later 1950's, by which time it was hardly worth the bother; the new goods shed quickly fell out of use and became a bus garage. The station remained much the same until the early 1980's, looking increasingly shabby and run down. The canopies were shortened, the curtain wall around the gents toilets was demolished, and with the derelict goods yard it did little to attract travellers.

Happily things looked up with rail privatisation and in 2012 the station was refurbished and in 2014 even gained a café on platform 1; the booking office is still staffed and the train service is the best it has ever been. There are regular Cross Country trains every hour, supplemented by East Midlands Trains services including one direct to St Pancras. The old goods yard was finally cleared to allow for the construction of the new council offices; the station environment has never looked better and this is reflected in the healthy passenger numbers.

The station in 1953 with a long freight train heading west. A building has been demolished in the goods yard since 1926, and in the foreground a cylindrical water softening plant has been erected by the wagon repair shops. The glass canopies are black, indicating how grimy things quickly became in the steam age. On the left the allotments still cover a huge area; this is now part of the park.

The station in about 1910, with much of the infrastructure in place that survives today. The walls are plastered with notices and adverts.

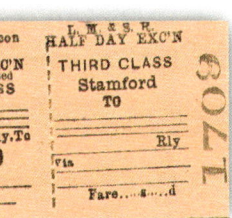

The scene in about 1960, grimy and uninviting even on this bright day. The Pedigree factory is taking shape in the distance.

It's hard to believe that the canopies are glass covered!

A long train of iron ore runs through the station in 1963. Horse boxes were a common sight in the hunting season.

A train from Great Yarmouth at Melton in 1934 behind M&GNR No. 2

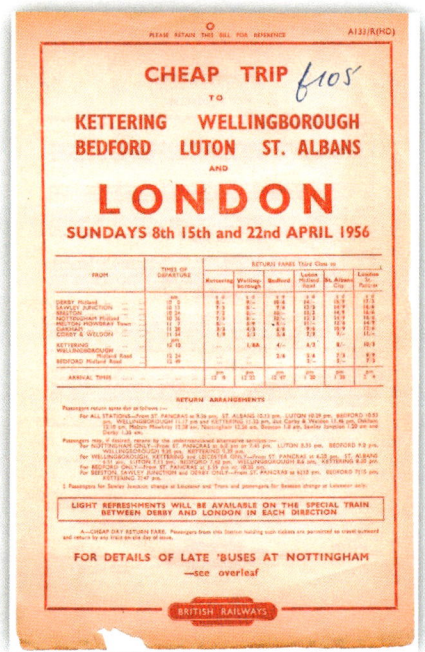

Another freight train trundles through the station; on the right is the former crossing keepers cottage.

How things have changed! Two pictures taken in 2011 when the station was in the middle of a major refurbishment. The signalling is still pretty much from the steam age, though.

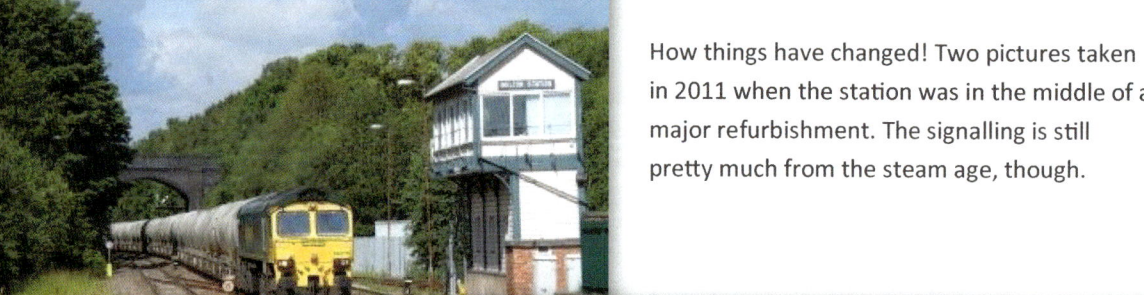

East of Melton station on the four tracked section, a 4F hauled train heads towards the M&GN line and the Norfolk coast. The M&GN line closed in 1959 ending scenes such as this. The picture was taken from a footbridge which allows a footpath to cross the line...all the fields on the left are now covered with houses.

By 1982 the loops had been shortened, the trains were less interesting, and the houses had begun to encroach. The Pedigree factory had grown out of all recognition.

This is the same site in 2012. The footbridge had just been replaced with a new structure.

MELTON MOWBRAY JOINT STATION (LATER MELTON MOWBRAY NORTH).

The lesser known station in Melton was a later addition, opening in 1879, and it closed to normal passenger traffic as early as 1953.

Two major railway companies, the Great Northern and the London and North Western, wanted to challenge the monopoly enjoyed by the Midland Railway in this part of Leicestershire so they combines forces to build a line to run south from the GNR route from Nottingham to Grantham. The route ran due south to Melton, then turned west before running south again to end at a junction with the LNWR line between Rugby and Peterborough. A branch owned just by the GNR served Leicester.

The problem with the route was that other than Melton it didn't serve any towns, all the stations serving isolated villages which were never going to generate much traffic. Freight traffic was important, especially when iron ore deposits around Scalford and Waltham were exploited, but despite the lavish station at Melton passenger receipts remained poor. The problem was that you could travel from Melton in any direction more conveniently over the Midland routes, to Leicester, Peterborough or Nottingham. There were more trains, and they were much quicker. Melton Joint was a station without a real purpose as far as passengers were concerned.

The line opened on September 1st 1879 to goods and passenger traffic to Nottingham London Road, and on December 15th for the routes to Grantham, Newark and south towards Peterborough & Rugby. To begin with the LNWR laid on trains from Northampton to Nottingham or Newark, and the GNR trains that began at Melton and ran to Grantham, the only route not already provided by the Midland. The through train to Newark was so poorly used that it was withdrawn on 1st May 1882, and when the GNR line to Leicester Belgrave Road opened on 1st January 1883 the GNR service became Grantham to Leicester via Melton.

The problem was that Melton just wasn't a big enough place to justify all these different trains; in 1910 the direct Newark service was down to one train a day, and it ended in 1922.

The station was renamed Melton North when British Railways was formed in 1948. The regular scheduled passenger service finished on 7th December 1953 but holiday specials from Leicester to Skegness, always a success, continued to run and call at Melton until the end of the 1962 season. By then the track was not fit to be used for passenger trains. Goods traffic clung on until 1964.

The station site was cleared in 1970 and redeveloped and now it is difficult to imagine that it ever existed.

The Joint station in about 1900, far superior to the Midland station but sadly underused from the day it opened. Accommodation was lavish; the first class waiting rooms had heated toilet seats!

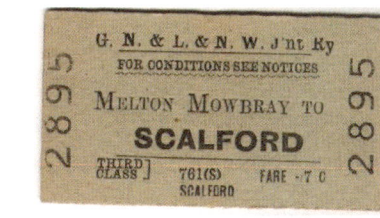

MELTON MOWBRAY JOINT STATION 1885

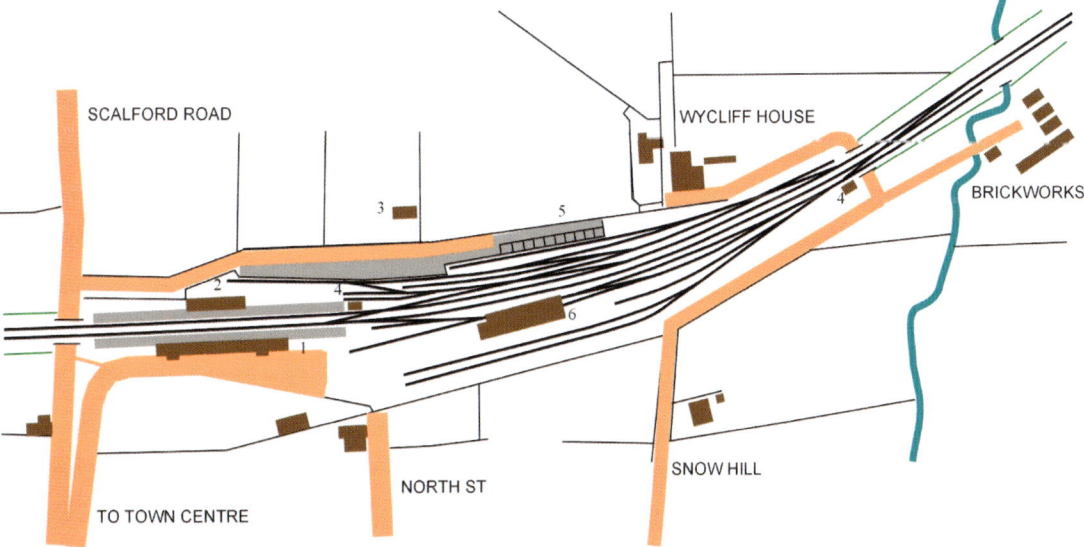

1 - MAIN STATION BUILDING 2 - NOTTINGHAM PLATFORM BUILDING 3 - WATER TANK
4 - SIGNAL BOX 5 - CATTLE PENS 6 - GOODS SHED.

The line approached Melton from the north east though what is now the country park, and curved to run west through the station. The goods yard was laid out in a far superior manner to the cramped arrangement at the Midland station, reflecting the later construction, and freight was always important at the joint station. A large brick goods shed had a track running directly to it, and there was ample siding space. Large cattle pens stood on the north side of the line, the proximity of the cattle market making his an important traffic.

The two platforms were flanked by red brick buildings connected by an underpass, with wide glazed canopies of a type not seen anywhere else. The station approach was from Scalford road, and the line crossed this on a metal girder bridge before curving south again.

The railway marked the northern edge of the town until well into the 1950's, the area south of the line being developed between 1880 and 1900.

The canopy glazing was removed as a safety measure during World War 2 and was never replaced, and the station was so little used it began to look very shabby.

A B1 class 4-6-0 runs through with a holiday train bound for Skegness in about 1960.

A service train shortly before the station closed in 1953, bound for Leicester. There was little to attract the traveller when the same journey could be done from the other station in less than half the time.

The station in 1953, showing how the area between the railway and the town was built up once the line had opened. Almost nothing seen on this picture remains today, the whole area was totally changed in the 1970's and 1980's. The two gables of the old Egerton brewery can be seen and that building is still there on North Street which helps orientate the picture.

The goods yard in 1926, with a locomotive shunting. Empty iron ore hopper wagons can be seen, probably waiting to be taken to Waltham, and in the foreground are the cattle pens. On the left is Wycliff House, almost the only development in this area at the time. Now the built up area stretches far north of here.

A holiday excursion returning to Leicester runs out of the station and crosses Scalford Road bridge in the mid 1950's.

The attractive station building seen from the approach road.

The last freight train, in 1964. The track was in a deplorable state, no wonder the holiday trains had to be withdrawn.

Dereliction. The site was cleared in 1970.

MELTON JUNCTION.

The railway map of the town changed dramatically in 1879/80, from the single line between Syston and Peterborough to having a second station and two direct links to Nottingham. To the west of the town lay Melton Junction, where these routes connected.

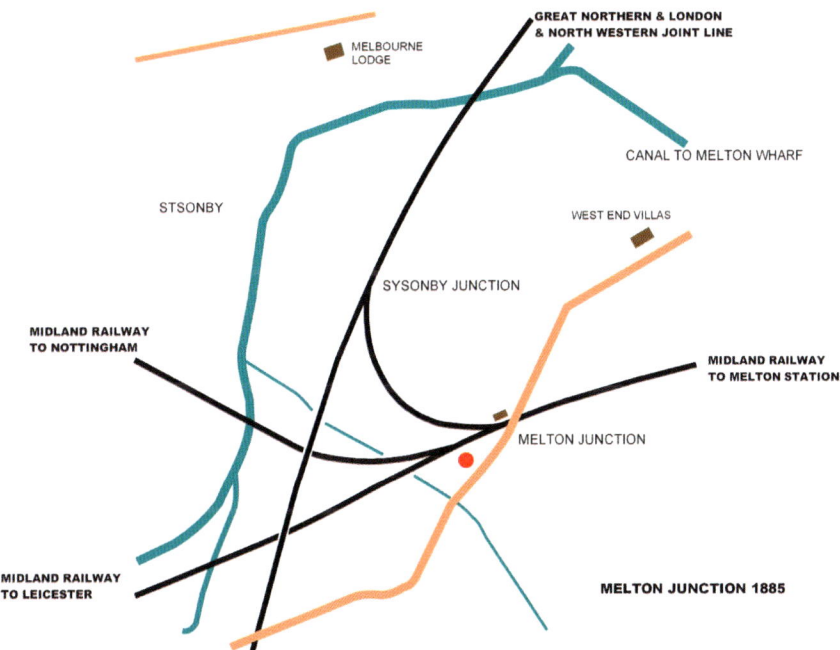

This map shows the arrangement of the junctions soon after being opened. The original MR line of 1846 runs right to left with Melton Midland station off the map to the right. The road is Leicester Road.

The GNR & LNWR joint line opened in 1879 runs from top to bottom, with Melton Joint station of the map to the to right.

The third route is the new Midland main line to Nottingham, which branches off the original route and runs towards the to left, creating Melton Junction. This opened on 1st November 1879 to goods and to passengers on 2nd February 1880.

A connecting loop was built between the two routes so that freight traffic could be exchanged but it was little used, partly because relations between the MR and the Joint line were rather frosty! It opened on the opening of the joint line in 1879 but was closed and severed in 1882, only to be replaced in 1883 and then closed for good in 1887. There would have been a small signal box at Sysonby Junction, one of the shortest lived ever built.

This area was open country in 1885, indeed it remained so until well into the second half of the twentieth century. Now it looks very different; to allow you to work out what was where, the red dot marks the site of B&Q.

A holiday excursion on the Joint line returning to Leicester behind a B1 locomotive crosses the Midland lines at Melton junction; the Midland sidings can be seen on the right. The date is about 1960, towards the end of the passenger excursions to Leicester.

A Class 25 diesel loco passes beneath the bridge seen in the top picture in 1970, just before the bridge was removed. By this time the Nottingham line had closed, and it lay unused for some years before gaining new life as the Old Dalby test track.

An eastbound freight on the Midland line passes Melton Junction signal box behind a 4F locomotive. The train is about to pass under the Leicester Road bridge.

An eastbound freight behind a J39 locomotive passes under the Joint line bridge in 1958, an everyday sight but an unusual class of engine on the Midland route. The train was Leicester to March which explains the Eastern locomotive.

Photo by HN James, used with permission.

An LMS passenger train to Leicester passes under the Leicester Road bridge in 1936 behind a Midland Compound loco. The vehicle behind the engine is a 6 wheeled milk tank.

The bridge was replaced in 2011 with a much wider modern structure.

Photo by HN James, used with permission.

The view from Leicester Road bridge in 1982, showing the Nottingham line reduced to a single track. All the fields in this picture have now been built over; that on the left houses B&Q.

The signal box stood in the foreground to the right of the main line. The row of bushes marks the route of the Sysonby loop line.

CHAPTER 10

HUNTING AND THE HUNT LODGES.

Whether you consider it to be the 'unspeakable in pursuit of the inedible' or the most civilizing influence since sliced bread, there is not getting away from the fact that fox hunting has moulded the town of Melton in a way that no other influence has come close to. Had hunting not taken to Melton in the way it did the architecture of the town would be much poorer, and pork pies may never have become the food of choice for the highest in the land.

The story begins with the formation of the Quorn hunt in 1753 which is when fox hunting became an organised activity rather than just a group of farmers trying to keep their chickens safe. Several other hunts were soon developed in the same region, notably the Belvoir and the Cottesmore. Melton lay right in the middle of the triangle they formed, so it was natural that the town became the centre for the hunts and the social activities associated with them. They even spilt the town into areas; the Belvoir claimed Nottingham Street and Sherrard Street, the Cottesmore claimed Burton Street and the Quorn the Leicester Road side of town....it was like football club rivalry today.

The hunts attracted the cream of the Aristocracy, who hunted hard by day and lived hard by night which wasn't always to the benefit of the town as a whole. This was a seasonal activity, beginning in November and lasting through the winter months so there was some respite!

Among the more notable visitors was the Prince of Wales, son of George 3rd who would become King George in his turn. He visited he town several times, staying at Belvoir Castle and hunting with the Belvoir pack. He gained a reputation for meanness in the town, never giving a tip, and resentment grew to the extent that he was once pelted with snowballs.

PAINTING THE TOWN RED.

The most famous expression connected with Melton also has it's origins in this period. In the 1830's the Marquis of Waterford was a young man with too much money and time on his hands, and he and a group of cronies caused havoc wherever they went; being aristocracy, of course, little could be done to stop them. Melton had the misfortune to be one of their favourite haunts.

After a day at the Croxton Park races on April 6th 1837, following an excellent dinner and no doubt several bottle of stimulant they rampaged through the town at 3am, breaking down the tollgates at Thorpe End where they came across some tins of bright red paint. They first screwed up the shutters on the toll-house and screwed the door shut, then they headed off down Thorpe End taking the tins of paint with them.

All along Sherrard Street they painted doors red, broke plant pots and daubed the shop fronts; then they came to the market place. Standing proudly alongside the road was the Sawn Inn, and the temptation proved too much. Above the front of the in was a carved stone swan, and the group hoisted the Marquis up so that he could paint the swan bright red. They then carried on along Burton Street, throwing pub signs into the canal and breaking windows, so they weren't concerned about drawing attention to themselves. This not surprisingly is what they did, when two of the group were grabbed by two Police officers.

One of the two escaped but the other was locked into an impromptu cell, the room of a nearby cottage. The rest of the gang then threatened to kill the officers if they didn't hand over the key, which sensibly is what they did; the man was quickly freed.

The following morning Melton awoke to find a town adorned; and to make it worse by now the paint had dried so removing it was even harder.

Something had to be done; special constables were sworn in, and they were needed because the following evening the same group were out causing havoc again, threatening to fight the constables. One of the group was arrested and this time he was retained in custody. He was bound over to keep the peace for £200, a huge sum in 1837, and told to compensate the constables and an injured watchman.

Arrest warrants were issued for the whole group, and they were brought before the assizes in Leicester. They were found not guilty, but were fined £100 each. Some put it down to high spirits, but many in Melton were less willing to forgive and of course the incident has never been forgotten.

Whether that is truly the origin of the phrase 'paint the town red' is open to conjecture, but certainly Melton seems to have as good a claim as anywhere else.

THE MIDNIGHT STEEPLECHASE.

The second incident that has lived on in local memory is the Midnight Steeplechase, another drunken revel. Fifty years after the time of the Marquis, the idea arose among the young men of the hunt to honour his memory and on March 19th 1890 that is what they did.

They began by donning full hunting regalia and set off along Sherrard Street on horseback, waking the town as they went by singing 'A hunting we will go' at top volume. Reaching the Old Club on Burton Street, they went inside to where a party was being held and eight young men donned ladies clothes over their hunting gear. At 11pm they set off for The Spinneys where a mile long course had been laid out. Oil lamps from the station had been purloined to light the course but it was still incredibly dangerous; only two of the eight finished the mile. Major Burnaby won a cup and £50 for winning the race.

Then it was back into town to celebrate, of course, with much noise, blowing of horns and singing. Next to the Old Club, to which they returned, was the residence of the Vicar of Melton and he was not at all impressed!

His sermon the following Sunday was a fierce one, but there don't seem to have been any legal sanctions against the participants.

This is Thorpe End tollhouse from which the red paint was stolen and the gate broken. The painting looks to be a rather romanticised version!

Now to the market place and the Swan Inn!

Here is the famous swan, back in place following the dreadful fire that destroyed the building in 1985.

Some have doubted the veracity of the story of the red paint, but when the swan was taken down traces of red paint were found on the back of it.

There is a connection between the huntsmen and the Melton pork pie because the huntsmen wanted something to take with them that they could eat, and only the pork pie was able to withstand the rigours of the journey! It could be slipped into a pocket, was filling and easy to hold and filled the bill perfectly. Word spread, and it soon became a staple food, also being used for picnics at the local race meetings.

HUNTING LODGES AND THE OLD CLUB

The aristocratic visitors to Melton didn't want to mix with the common people in the hotels and inns, so they made other arrangements. Money being no object, a number of large houses began to spring up around the town which were used in the winter months as a base from which to go hunting. These were the hunting lodges and many of them remain.

Before that, though, there was the 'Old Club' on Burton Street, which became the hub of the social life for the hunting set. It was built in about 1790 to provide a centre for the hunting fraternity and became the hub of their social life despite only having four bedrooms.

The Old Club is on the right in this winter view looking towards the market place.

The building remains but the ground floor has been converted into shops.

People wanted their own place to stay rather than hiring a room in a club, so the hunting lodges came into being, large houses in grounds on the edges of the town. These were the first houses built south of the river.

They included Newport Lodge, home of the Laycocks, Wicklow Lodge, home to the Fenwicks, Staveley Lodge, home to the Lawsons, Wyndham Lodge, home to the Chaplins, Craven Lodge, home to the Baldocks, Egerton Lodge and the Wilton family and several others including the Spinneys and Coventry House by the canal.

The family would move in for the hunting season, and they would be left empty over the Summer ...this way of life persisted until 1914, but things were never the same after that.

Craven Lodge before and after the recent restoration. These houses were huge, much to big to be used as a home in modern times.

Craven Lodge operated as a club between the wars, with members including Edward Prince of Wales, but after 1945 it was unable to reopen.

After failing to find a buyer at Auction in 1928, Egerton Lodge became the council offices and remained so for forty years. It is now a residential home.

Most of these houses ended up as schools, offices or being split up into apartments. Wyndham Lodge was given to the town and became the War Memorial Hospital.

The postcards show Staveley Lodge and Egerton Lodge.

JOHN FERNELEY

Melton was blessed by having two talented artists living in the town at the time when hunting was at it's height. The first was John Fernely.

He was born in 1782 in Thrussington, and although he was at first apprenticed as a master wheelwright, his fathers trade, he was encouraged to develop his clear artistic talent by no less a person than the Duke of Rutland. He moved to London to study, and joined the Royal Academy School. He exhibited, travelled to Ireland, but then returned to live in Melton when he married. His house and studio was Elgin Lodge on Scalford Road and was the place to be seen; he kept open house for his wealthy clients.

Ferneley was in the right place at the right time; he specialised in painting horses and his clients included the Royal family, Beau Brummel and most of the hunting aristocracy. He painted all the local hunts, and travelled again to Ireland to fulfil commissions there. His first wife died in 1836; they had six children of whom three became painters.

Ferneley died in 1860, and John Ferneley College is named after him.

Ferneley's painting of two hunters belonging to Sir John Thorold; his horses looked natural, he had the knack of capturing their stance so they don't look stiff like the work of some of his contemporaries.

FRANCIS GRANT

Grant is the second of Melton's great artists, and was a friend of Ferneley. He was born in 1803 so he was twenty one years younger but Ferneley was perfectly happy to take tuition from the younger man as well as offering it himself. Grant was born in Perthshire and educated at Harrow school. He inherited a fortune on the death of his father in 1818 though seemingly it was 'soon spent'. He loved fox hunting and so was drawn to Melton. He was a self taught painter, but his talent was obvious.

Like Ferneley he gained a reputation for painting sporting subjects, though he was a more skilled painter of people. He painted 'the Melton Hunt' in 1839, perhaps his introduction to the town.

After 1840 Grant concentrated on painting portraits, including Queen Victoria, and in 1866 he became president of the Royal Academy; he was knighted shortly afterwards.

Grant's home was The Lodge in Melton, and he died there after some years of poor health in 1878. he was buried in Melton churchyard, his family turning down the offer of a burial at St Pauls cathedral.

Never mind Queen Victoria, this is the picture the town of Melton holds dear! Titled 'the Melton Breakfast' it shows the interior of the Old Club and was painted in 1834, an early work that was engraved and so reached a wide audience.

Other notable personages were to be seen in Melton during the nineteenth century. Lord Cardigan, who ordered the Charge of the Light Brigade, lived in Cardigan House and hunted regularly. His wife long out-lived him and used to scandalise the Victorian Meltonians by sitting on her balcony with her face painted and powdered in a way that no lady was supposed to do!

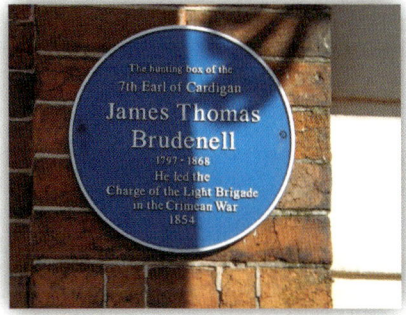

The house is now the offices of Denmans builders, a very long established Melton firm, and is kept in very good condition.

Hunting flourished before the First World War, and again into the 1930's but after that began to decline and the days of Melton being in the centre of social life were over. Famous visitors still arrived ,though; the Prince of Wales and as he then became King Edward 7th, and then from 1923 onwards Edward Prince of Wales. He stayed at Craven Lodge and called Melton his second home; he could be free here, unlike in London. He had several relationships with married women, carried out quietly at Craven Lodge, and then he met Wallace Simpson. Much of their courtship took place around Melton, and lead of course to his ab-dication in 1936.

Winston Churchill also visited Melton in the years before 1914, but he was not too popular with the other huntsmen as he was a member of the government that had just increased income tax!

CHAPTER 11

THE TOWN ESTATE

The Melton Mowbray Town Estate dates back to the fourteenth century as is very much a unique survivor that has done much to give the modern town it's character.

In Medieval times Guilds, originally begun for religious reasons, grew up to represent different trades and professions. They grew wealthy due to inheriting property and money, and in line with that their power increased, many of them taking over the functions of local government such as education. During the Dissolution of the Monasteries in the time of Henry 8th, the power of the Guilds was also reined in and much of their wealth confiscated. This impacted locally, a house in the town being given to Thomas Cromwell and then following his execution to Anne of Cleves.

The Town Estate came into being as a way of continuing the good work of the Guilds without creating problems with the King. The local Guilds were St Johns and St Marys, and they ran a school in the town among other things. The Church provided the money to set up the Town Estate by selling silver and plate belonging to the Church (perhaps done so that the king couldn't remove it), and buying the first land to belong to the Estate.

The first written records date from 1549, when *'a parcel of land with appertances lately called the chapel house in Melton bought of the Town of Melton use'*. Nicholas Colishaw was the Church warden and it was he who arranged the sale for the price of £21.00. The piece of land was roughly where the present cattle market lies, and twenty local men were appointed as trustees for the benefit of the town and the school. Income from the land was in the form of rents and levies, which paid for the upkeep of the school.

An area of land called The Spinneys (shown on the 1500 map, north of the town towards Beck Mill) was bought in 1564 bringing in more revenue. By 1575 there was the original free school and a grammar school, pretty progressive for the time. In 1582 the twenty trustees were reduced to twelve, with two Townwardens, a post that has existed ever since.

By this point he Town Estate was acting much as a modern council does, running local services and keeping he town maintained. It had taken over the upkeep of the roads and bridges by 1582 (indicating that the fords had fallen out of use by then), and by the end of the century it owned several properties. And large areas of grazing land.

The rights of the Lord of the Manor of Melton Mowbray were purchased in 1850 for £650 allowing the Estate to take over the running of the street markets and to generate income from them.

The original land bought to set up the Estate was leased to the Local Government Board in 1869 for £50 per annum, useful income for a period of the lease of 999 years.

Today the Town Estate owns the following:

Play Close, bought for £170 in 1866. This was enlarged in 1872 and 1886.

A paddock in Leicester Street bought for £200.

Leicester Road sports ground bought for £400.

The gardens of Egerton Lodge, bought in 1929 for £500.

Saxby Road sports ground was given to the Estate in 1949 by the Bickley Trust.

The site in King Street of the new college was rented to the County Council for five shillings per annum in 1936.

Asfordby Road golf course, the land being bought in 1972 with proceeds from land on Dalby Road being sold.

Priors Close was presented to the town by Pedigree Petfoods in 1986.

Land on Kirby Lane, Dalby Road and Nottingham Road.

Land on Windsor Street and Chapel Street.

The 'Glory Hole' at the back of Wilton Road car park.

The Town Baliffs Cottage, Park Lane, the offices of the Town Estate.

CHAPTER 12

THE CATTLE MARKET AND STREET MARKET.

Originally a market was just a convenient place to come and sell things, a particular spot where people selling the same goods could gather. It made sense for this to be in a central location, so market towns grew up, and it made sense for that spot to be marked in some way so market crosses were erected.

Markets in those days had no buildings; you took your chances with the weather! In Melton as far back as records go the market was on a Tuesday, and all the local farmers would come to town to buy and sell produce and animals. Stalls would be erected in some places by the more professional, and hurdles were used to create pens to keep the animals in one place. There would be noise, smell, mess, dirt and something of a festival atmosphere if the weather was good because this may be the only time in the week that people were able to get away for a few hours, whether buying or selling. Gossip would be exchanged and no doubt the taverns did a roaring trade.

This was the pattern of things until well into the nineteenth century. Different areas of the town were used for selling different things as it made sense to keep the cattle away from the cheese, for instance.

Beginning at the north end of town, the visitor would first encounter the sheep market on Nottingham Street, then at the top of High Street was the corn market. Butter and other dairy produce including piles of cheeses were sold in the market place at the High Cross, and then came the beast market in Sherrard Street where mainly cattle were sold. Further along at the end of Sage Cross Street were stalls selling herbs for medicines, and possibly salt at the end of Thorpe End which was originally called Saltgate. In between would be other stalls selling shoes, cloth, household implements, anything that could be transported to the town to be sold. An amazing 50,000 sheep were sold each year in Nottingham Street.

Fairs were held during the year in addition to the normal market: the ones in Whit week and on St Lawrence day are ancient, while three more were nineteenth century additions of which the Stilton Cheese Fair was the most important by far.

However, by the mid 1800's there began to be complaints about the selling of live animals in the town centre and the mess they left behind afterwards. Steps were taken to separate the livestock from the street market, and in 1870 a site was identified off Scalford Road. Here a purpose built market was constructed on land bought from the Town Estate which remains to this day. Lord Melbourne was Lord of the Manor and he owned the rights to the market and the fairs but he was happy to sell the rights to the Town Estate and so pass on the burden of all the organising.

The Scalford Road site was convenient because in 1879 the joint station was built nearby, making the transport of livestock a lot easier. The Midland station had been too far away to have been of use. Much stock was still walked to the market, but it could now travel by rail from further afield.

Market day in March 2015, a tradition with an unbroken history going back to Saxon times.

It's probably a good thing the cows and sheep have been moved out of town!

The 1870 buildings at the entrance to the cattle market; much of what is inside is modern but these buildings have been there since the market opened.

CHAPTER 13

MELTON IN THE TWENTIETH CENTURY.

At the beginning of the twentieth century Melton was a busy, prosperous town with good transport links, ample employment and a national reputation for its products. The town had a supply of gas and electricity, and was beginning to grow beyond the confines of the mid Victorian town with development along Thorpe Road, Saxby Road and Scalford Road. To the south and west though little new building had taken place other than the large hunting lodges of the wealthy.

Lady Wilton Bridge on Leicester Road pretty much marked the edge of the town in 1900, beyond the river it was fields and open countryside. The bridge was built in 1822, replacing an earlier structure which dated back to at least 1562, and was named after Lady Wilton who lived in nearby Egerton Lodge from 1856. Her husband died in 1885 leaving her childless but she was a popular society hostess and a benefactor to the town. The bridge is shown with gas lighting, later replaced with electric lights. To the left is a ramp leading down to the water, once used for soaking cart wheels to prevent then drying out and breaking.

The town centre looked much the same as in previous years; the market square was not the open space we know now, a block of shops known as the 'Barnes Block' filled the central area until it was demolished in 1963, the market stalls being erected along the streets and pavements and seriously restricting the flow of traffic which became an increasing problem as time went on.

S 10379   THORPE END AND LIBRARY, MELTON MOWBRAY.

Thorpe End in about 1910, showing newly installed electric street lighting.

Free Library, Melton Mowbray.

The Carnegie Library was opened in 1905 by which time the library had outgrown the old Bede house. It remained here until 1977 when it was relocated to the old girls school on Wilton Road, a far bigger premises, and the Carnegie building became the town museum.

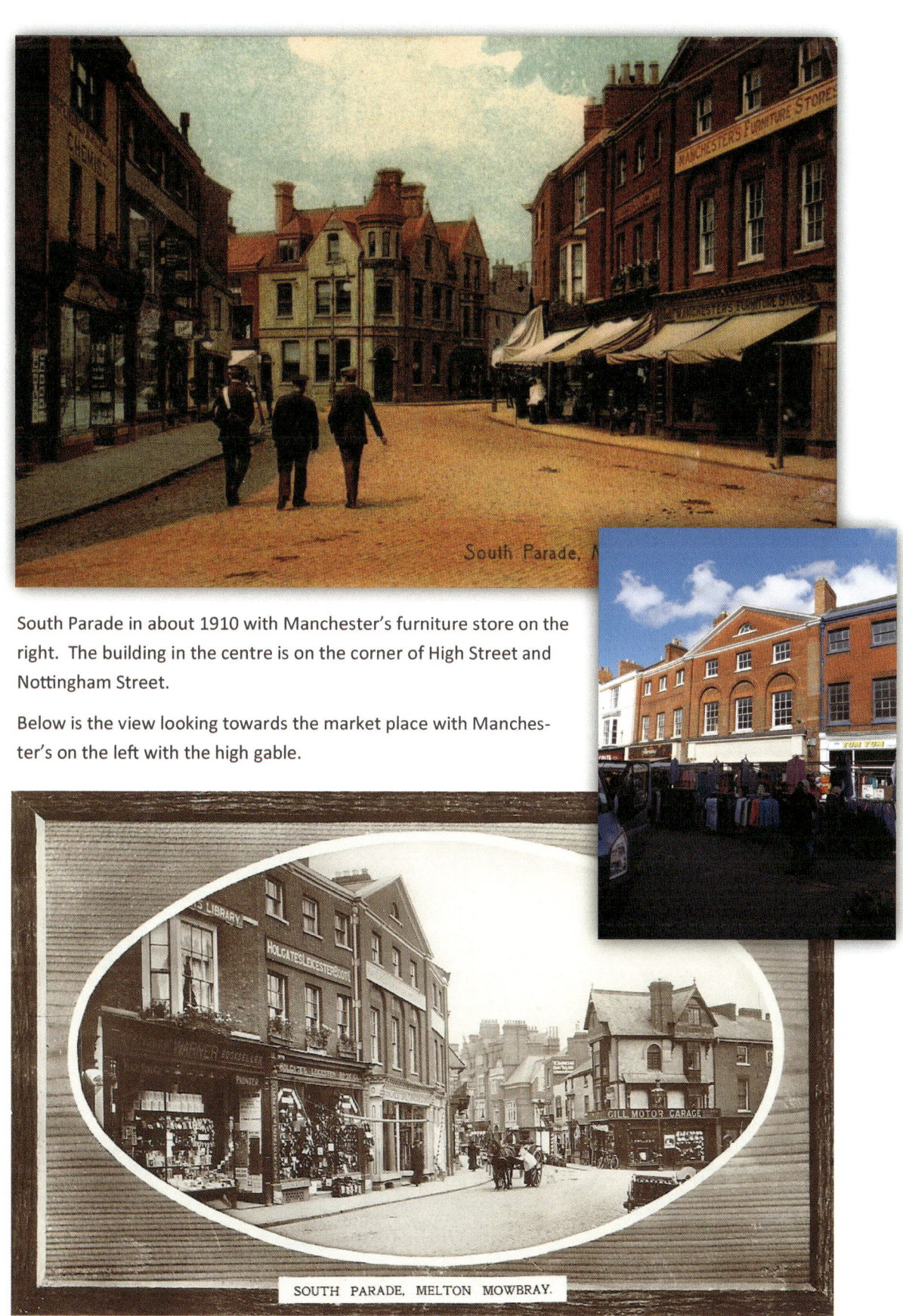

South Parade in about 1910 with Manchester's furniture store on the right. The building in the centre is on the corner of High Street and Nottingham Street.

Below is the view looking towards the market place with Manchester's on the left with the high gable.

SOUTH PARADE, MELTON MOWBRAY.

With the development of motor traffic the medieval road layout of Melton was beginning to be a serious bottleneck. All through traffic had to past through the town centre, which was a crossroads connecting routes to Leicester, Nottingham, Oakham and Grantham.

The first scheme to reduce the congestion was the construction of Wilton Road in 1933. Following the death of Lady Wilton in 1928 the council bought Egerton lodge and this allowed a small portion of the house to be demolished. This in turn allowed the construction of a straight road connecting the end of High Street and Leicester Street to Nottingham Road where a roundabout made a junction with Norman Street and Asfordby Road. In this way through traffic between Leicester and Nottingham could avoid the town centre altogether, greatly reducing congestion. A garage was built on the corner of High Street, and a large car park and bus station was laid out to the west of the new road. Finally, the Modern School for Girls was built next to the car park, opening in December 1933; the building is now the town library.

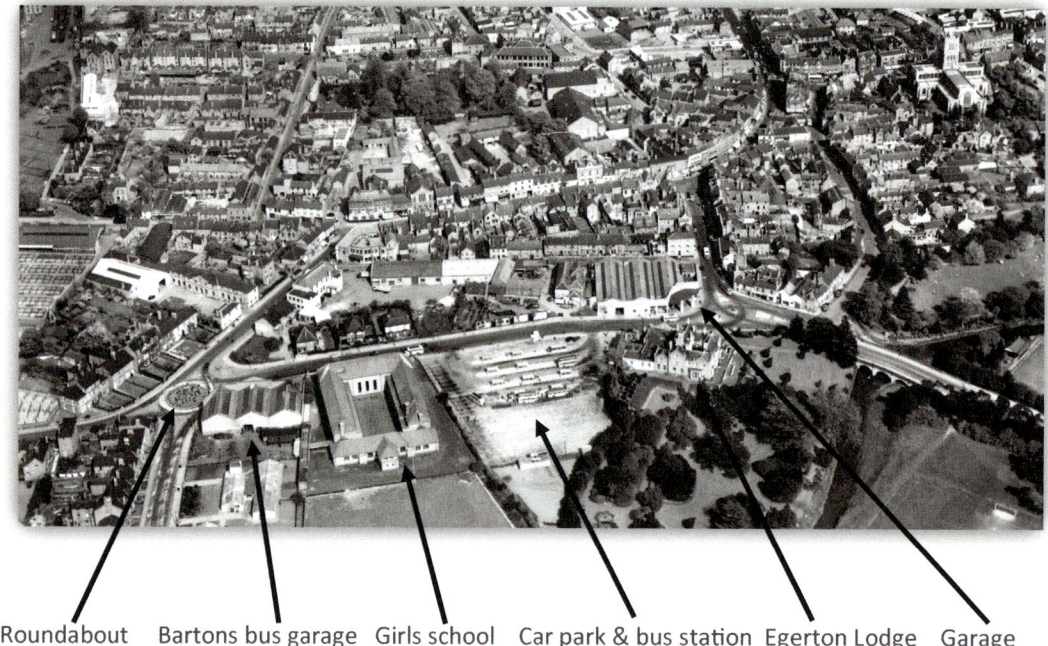

Roundabout   Bartons bus garage   Girls school   Car park & bus station   Egerton Lodge   Garage

A Midland Red service to Leicester at the Wilton Road bus station in the 1970's.

The Wilton Road area in 1953 with Egerton Lodge lower left and Garners Garage opposite; this is now a supermarket. The lack of traffic is noticeable compared with today; the car park is almost empty.

Picture courtesy of English Heritage.

Wilton Road was the only major improvement to the road system in Melton until Norman way was built in the early 1980's, which allowed the town centre to be pedestrianized. Melton still has a traffic problem, though; the layout of the streets is still basically medieval.

The hunt assembles in the market place in the 1950's, with WH Smiths in the background.

Burton Street in the motor age; the half timbered building on the left, now demolished, was a garage. The picture dates from the early 1960's but little here had changed for over a century.

Cheapside in the late 1930's with Boots on the left and the now demolished Barnes Block in the middle of the market place. Until Wilton Road was built in 1933 all through traffic had to past through here, including on Tuesdays when the market was in full swing.

This picture was taken in 1932, just before the new road was opened, and illustrates the problem even with the light traffic of those days. The Swan Porch is in the background, with the Melton Mowbray & District Farmer's Association' next door with the title painted on the front wall. The large shop on the left is Warner's store, a confectioners with a restaurant upstairs.

BARTON'S BUS GARAGE AND THE BUS STATION

The bus service to Oakham and Nottingham was provided by Bartons who had a bus garage on the corner of Wilton Road and Asfordby Road where the theatre and college now stands. It was built in 1933 when the new bus station was opened.

Above; the garage in 1984, not long before it was closed and demolished.

Two Barton vehicles in the garage in 1972.

The bus pick up points are now in St Mary's Way and the old bus station is used for more car parking.

FARROW & SONS MOTOR SERVICES.

Arthur Gordon Farrow, always known as Dick, started this business in 1919, first by running local bus services and the odd private hire and over the years this side of the business developed. In 1933 Arthur died leaving two sons Arthur and John, always called Jack. His widow Lillian ran the Pork Butchers shop at 11 Scalford Road, the shop also serving as the booking office for the bus/coach business. Arthur and Jack took over the running of the company operating out of the original garage in Pall Mall, Melton Mowbray. Over the years the company increased in size and required additional space and were able to purchase the adjoining Salvation Army Hall and house and the Dog & Gun public house to the right of Pall Mall Garage. They operated from these premises until 1972 when the Pall Mall depot was compulsory purchased for the development of flats. The firm moved to the disused joint station goods shed at the top of North Street remaining there until a new garage building was erected on the same site. Arthur Farrow died in 1978 and John Farrow died in 1979. The business was taken over by Peter Farrow, Jack's eldest son and Dennis Farrow, Arthur's eldest son. This partnership carried on until 1984 when Peter left the business, and it was then run by Dennis & Sue Farrow until it closed in 1994.

FAIRTAX COACHES

This company was begun by John Penniston as a taxi firm based in Thorpe End and later expanded into running bus services.   They took over the redundant goods shed at Melton Town station and until 1987 they ran town bus services and coach tours. In that year Fairtax was taken over by Midland Fox but continued to trade under the original name, competing with Bartons on the town routes. In 1990 the company was fully absorbed into Fox, which in turn became part of Arriva following deregulation.

John Penniston died in 2012.

The office of the otherwise demolished Midland Railway goods shed was used by Fairtax, with the bus garage in the goods shed built in around 1960.

ST MARY'S WAY

This new road was constructed to connect Sherrard Street with Norman Street at the same time as Wilton Road, in 1933, and involved the demolition of the Variety Stores.

MELTON MOWBRAY AIRFIELD.

This was opened in 1942 as RAF Melton Mowbray and was initially intended for aircraft maintenance. Sited in high ground to the south of the town on the road to Great Dalby it was an exposed site but well away from built up areas. The road was diverted to follow the perimeter of the airfield. The airfield was taken over by Transport Command and glider tugs flew from there during 1944.

Following the war the area was used as a camp for Polish air personnel prior to resettlement, and then from 1959 to 1963 it was a base for Thor missiles. The airfield was taken out of use in 1964 and is now largely open space with some small factory units.

The control tower, now demolished.

EDUCATION

There was a spate of new building during the middle part of the twentieth century, giving Melton a modern education system in purpose built buildings.

The first school in the town existed as early as 1347, and when the 1850 Education act came in requiring every child to be given a free school place Melton had already being doing that for three hundred years, a progressive place indeed.

A girls school was built on King Street in 1793 and a boys school adjacent to it in 1818; overcrowding lead to a new school being built on Norman Street in 1853.

In the early 20th century control of the town schools was handed over to the Local Education authority from the Town Estate, relieving the town of an administrative burden.

New schools opened throughout the town; The Central Boys School on Limes Avenue in 1928, (now Brownlow Primary), the Girls Modern School on Wilton Road in 1933, the County Technical College on King Street in 1937, and King Edward 7th Grammar on Burton Road in 1933.

In 1977 the school on Wilton Road was closed to become the library and a new school built on Burton Road, Sarcen School for Girls.

The Technical College building on King Street, with typical 1930's architecture that doesn't look out of place next to the cinema.

THE WAR MEMORIAL HOSPITAL.

The second hospital to open to serve Melton originated as a hunting lodge on the slopes of Ankle Hill, built when that was open ground.

The first house to be built south of Melton's River Eye, Hill House was built pre 1760 by Mr Hind, and let to the Earl and Countess of Chesterfield. In 1840 Colonel Charles Wyndham moved to Melton to follow his passion for foxhunting. Col Wyndham rented Hill House and renamed it Wyndham Lodge, in the hunting tradition.

In 1852 Col. Wyndham was made Governor of the Tower of London and vacated Melton, much to his regret. In 1869 the house was rented by William Chaplin, who subsequently purchased it in 1870. Chaplin preferred the location to the building, and had the entire house rebuilt in Wartnaby stone by R. Winter Johnson of Melton, in 1874. Chaplin lived in the house for some 30 years.

The house and 15 acres of parkland were then purchased by Col. Richard Dalgleish in 1920 who gifted it to the town; it then became Melton & District Cottage Hospital. At the time, the local authority was looking for a suitable memorial to honour those who had fallen during the Great War, so in 1921 Wyndham Lodge finally became Melton & District War Memorial Hospital.

In 1948 the Hospital was absorbed into the National Health Service, and has remained so until it was decided to group all services at the St Mary's site on Thorpe Road. The War Memorial hospital was closed in 2005 and for ten years has stood empty, the grounds overgrown. There are finally now plans to turn into retirement homes.

NORMAN WAY.

By the late 1970's the traffic problem in Melton was getting desperate; ideally a by-pass would have been built (we're still waiting!), but that was unaffordable. Instead a massive scheme was announced that involved clearing swathes of Victorian housing and rebuilding Norman Street as a through route connecting with Thorpe End, the new road to be renamed Norman Way. Hardly a building was left standing to the north of the new road, right up to the former joint railway line, the whole are being flattened and redeveloped, mostly for retail and light industry rather than housing.

I did my driving test in 1984 and vividly remember coming out of the test centre straight into the road works that would become Norman way. I passed first time; I think the examiner took the view that anyone that could cope with Norman Way under construction would have no trouble dealing with the rest of Melton! The hill start on Ankle Hill was a piece of cake after that.

The new road opened later that year and it has certainly improved matters but such a lot was lost in the process; looking at the old pictures it hardly seems possible that it's the same town. There is simply nothing left in the area north of the new road that dates from before about 1980 other than the old brewery building on North Street. It was a community; almost overnight that disappeared.

One building that did survive the rebuilding work was the Magistrates Court, though at the time of writing the building was no longer in use. The width of the new road compared with the old Norman Street is very noticeable.

THE ROYAL ARMY VETERINARY CORPS AND THE DEFENCE ANIMAL CENTRE.

The town of Melton is rightly proud to be the home of the RAVC, the branch of the British Army responsible for the training and care of animals.

The department was formed in1796 after public outrage about the treatment of horses in the Army. Not until then was the first veterinary surgeon commissioned to care for the animals on which the Army then totally depended.

For the first 82 years of its existence the veterinary service in the army was organised entirely on a regimental basis. Veterinary surgeons were directly recruited into cavalry regiments and wore the uniform of the regiments they joined. There was no provision for the care of sick or lame horses when regiments were on the move and sick animals were either abandoned or became stragglers at the rear. The Peninsular War was the first time that an attempt was made to deal with this problem and sick horse depots were established.

In the aftermath of World War Two, the RAVC was involved in many countries, notably Germany, Austria, Greece, Burma and Malaya, in the disposal of surplus animals, the prevention of the spread of disease and animal husbandry. The RAVC also required a permanent depot and moved to the old Remount Depot at Melton Mowbray.

The RAVC did not fall to pre-war levels as World War Two had highlighted the role of dogs, which took over from horses and mules as the main military animal (the last operational pack transport unit was eventually disbanded in Hong Kong in 1976 although recent operations in Afghanistan have questioned the need for pack transport in difficult terrain). In Malaya and Borneo, during the 1950s and 1960s, dogs worked as tracker dogs seeking out insurgents. In Northern Ireland dogs have worked as arms and explosive search dogs seeking out terrorist arms and explosives, a role they are also carrying out in Iraq, and in Hong Kong dogs were trained to detect and apprehend illegal immigrants. However the main role is still one of protection reducing the number of soldiers needed for guard duties. The RAVC has permanent dog units in Northern Ireland, England, Germany and Cyprus.

The RAVC is one of the smallest Corps in the British Army yet provides invaluable support to the Army's animals and serves worldwide with them today.

In 2015 the centre mainly deals with horses and dogs, but there are also various regimental mascots to be cared for. The base is known as the Defence Animal Centre and dogs are trained for the RAF and the RN as well as the Army. It was established in Melton in 1946 and has continued to develop; an indoor riding school was opened in 2008 by Princess Anne.

Dogs are also trained for use by the UK Immigration Service, the HM Prison Service, HM Revenue & Customs and also other countries such as Ireland marking the recognition of Melton as a centre of excellence. The dogs are mainly Springer Spaniels, Labradors and Belgian Shepherds and they train to detect drugs and explosives. Around three hundred dogs are taken on each year and take up to six months to train fully.

CHAPTER 14

HOTELS AND HOSTELRIES

Before the eighteenth century when there was nothing to mark Melton out as any different from hundreds of other small market towns, public houses as we know them were unknown. There would have been small ale-houses, serving beer brewed on the premises, but little more. Beer is a heavy, bulky low value product and transporting it any distance was out of the question.

This began to change when the canal network developed, which in the case of Melton meant in 1797 when the River Wreake was made navigable through to the Soar. Suddenly it was possible to bring in barrels of beer from Burton on Trent and elsewhere, to import wine and spirits in bulk and thus to offer a much wider range of drinks to the public. The alehouses began to develop into what we would now recognise as public houses.

At the same time the three large Hotels were opened to serve the new scheduled road coaches that began to serve the town using the network of toll roads. These needed to change horses a regular intervals and the passengers need to be accommodated overnight as journeys could last several days. The George, the Bell and the Harborough all grew up to serve this trade, with stables behind the hotels. This is turn brought employment to the town, and made Melton accessible. When hunting developed at around the same time the presence of the hotels made the sport possible as large numbers of people were attracted, not just from the local area. These in turn required refreshment and entertainment and so in the first half of the nineteenth century a remarkable number of pubs were opened. By 1885 there were forty seven pubs & hotels in the town centre, serving a resident population of only 4500 which was a pub or hotel to every 95 people, including children.

Clearly they were not all making money just from the townspeople, but from visitors on market days, the hunting fraternity and others from outside the town. Even so it was not sustainable and the numbers began to drop over the ensuing decades. Two breweries also opened to serve the town, situated in North Street & Thorpe End, and the Crown Inn carried a large painted sign on the front advertising 'Celebrated Mowbray Ales'.

Burton Street in about 1910, with on the right the Harborough Hotel and to the right of that the thatched Red Lion Inn. Note the large opening below the bay window of the Harborough, through which the coaches would be driven in order to change horses in the hotel yard.

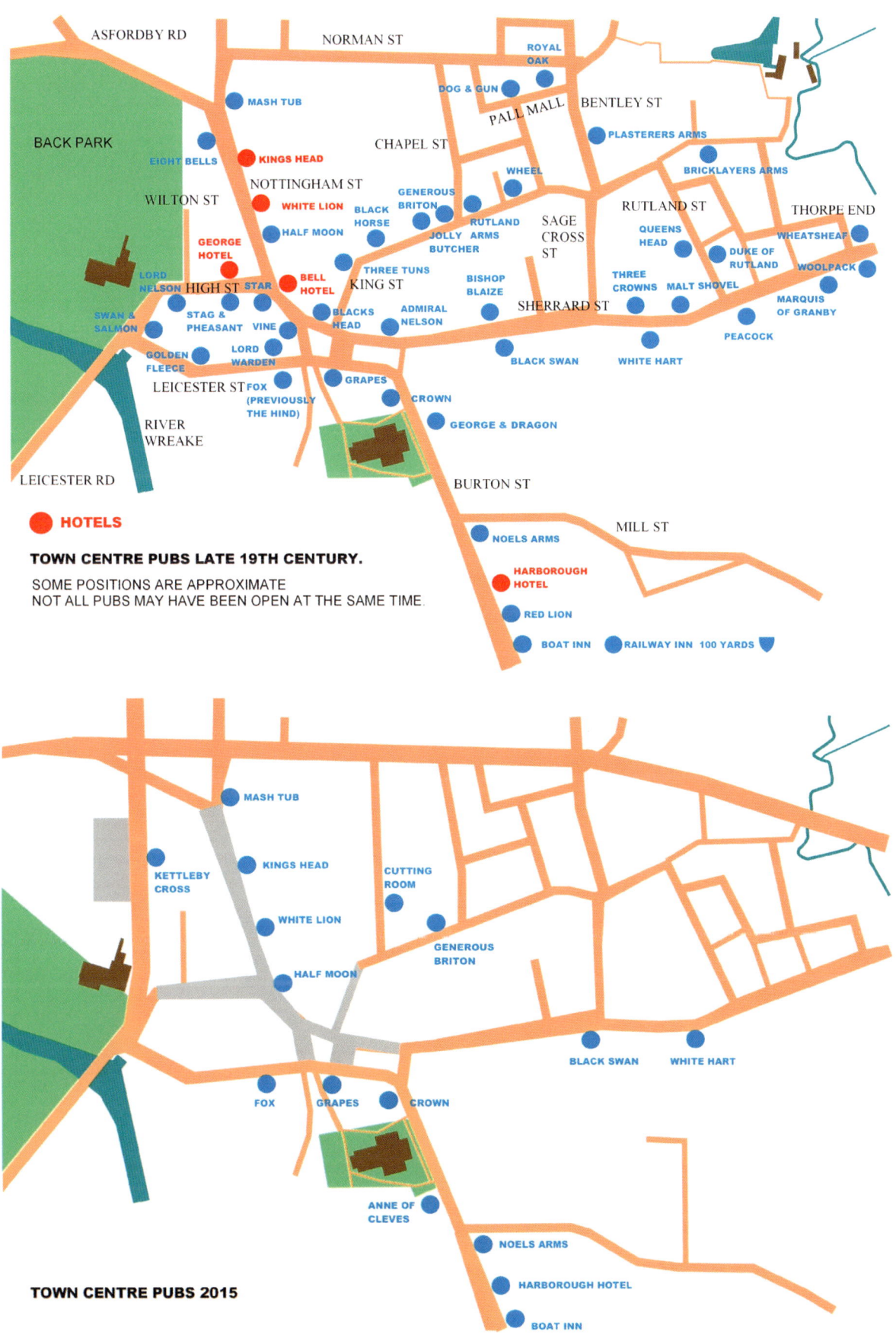

ASFORDBY RD   NORMAN ST

ROYAL OAK

DOG & GUN

BACK PARK   PALL MALL   BENTLEY ST

MASH TUB

PLASTERERS ARMS

CHAPEL ST

EIGHT BELLS   KINGS HEAD

WHEEL   BRICKLAYERS ARMS

NOTTINGHAM ST

WILTON ST   WHITE LION   GENEROUS BRITON   RUTLAND ST   THORPE END

BLACK HORSE   RUTLAND   SAGE CROSS ST   QUEENS HEAD   WHEATSHEAF

HALF MOON   JOLLY ARMS BUTCHER   DUKE OF RUTLAND   WOOLPACK

GEORGE HOTEL   THREE TUNS   KING ST   THREE CROWNS   MALT SHOVEL

LORD NELSON   HIGH ST   STAR   BELL HOTEL   BISHOP BLAIZE   MARQUIS OF GRANBY

SWAN & SALMON   STAG & PHEASANT   VINE   BLACKS HEAD   ADMIRAL NELSON   SHERRARD ST   PEACOCK

GOLDEN FLEECE   LORD WARDEN   WHITE HART

LEICESTER ST   FOX (PREVIOUSLY THE HIND)   GRAPES   BLACK SWAN

RIVER WREAKE   CROWN

LEICESTER RD   GEORGE & DRAGON

BURTON ST   MILL ST

● HOTELS

NOELS ARMS

TOWN CENTRE PUBS LATE 19TH CENTURY.

HARBOROUGH HOTEL

SOME POSITIONS ARE APPROXIMATE
NOT ALL PUBS MAY HAVE BEEN OPEN AT THE SAME TIME.

RED LION

BOAT INN   RAILWAY INN   100 YARDS ▼

MASH TUB

KETTLEBY CROSS   KINGS HEAD   CUTTING ROOM

WHITE LION

GENEROUS BRITON

HALF MOON

BLACK SWAN   WHITE HART

FOX   GRAPES   CROWN

ANNE OF CLEVES

NOELS ARMS

TOWN CENTRE PUBS 2015

HARBOROUGH HOTEL

BOAT INN

PUBS IN THE LATE NINETEENTH CENTURY.

This list covers all the pubs serving to town centre, many of which are still in business. Pubs that have since closed are shown in red.

THE MASH TUB On Nottingham Street close to the junction with Park Road.

THE EIGHT BELLS On Nottingham Street, it was the meeting place of the Fire Brigade when the alarm was raised. Closed in 1924.

THE KINGS HEAD On Nottingham Street, it was a coaching inn in 1885 advertising to the hunting set. Later owned by Home Ales.

THE WHITE LION A hotel in 1885, also on Nottingham Street. The trustees of the Melton to Grantham turnpike met here, as did the Society for the Prosecution of Felons.

THE HALF MOON On Nottingham Street opposite the end of High Street.

THE GREEN DRAGON On Nottingham Street, but position unknown (possibly where the Chapel was later built).

THE SWAN & SALMON On High Street opposite Egerton Lodge, close to the river.

THE STAR On High Street close to the junction with Nottingham Street.

STAG & PHEASANT On High Street but site uncertain.

LORD NELSON On High Street.

THE GOLDEN FLEECE On Leicester Street, it closed in the mid 1990's and is now a restaurant. The original building was thatched but was rebuilt in the later 1800's.

THE FOX On Leicester Street—previously called **THE HIND**. The building is old, possible 17th century.

THE LORD WARDEN On Leicester Street, it closed in 1908.

THE GRAPES The Grapes used to be the tap of the Swan Inn which closed in 1825, since when the Grapes has run independently. It was known locally as the 'Corner Cupboard'.

THE ADMIRAL NELSON On the north side of the Market Square.

THE BLACKS HEAD On the north side of the Market Place, it closed in 1939.

THE VINE On Butchers Row, Marketplace. It closed in 1914.

THE CROWN On Burton Street, just off the market square. In 1885 it offered 'Celebrated Mowbray Ales'.

THE NOELS ARMS On the corner of Mill Street and Burton Street.

GEORGE & DRAGON On Burton St on the site of the Collis Hall (1890), it was demolished in the 1870's.

THE RED LION This thatched pub stood next to the Harborough Hotel on Burton Street; it closed in 1928 and was demolished in 1930.

THE BOAT Built to serve the canal wharves in around 1797.

THE THREE TUNS On King Street, in the 1890's it housed a small brewery. There is an 1898 date stone but the building is eighteenth century.

THE BLACK HORSE On King Street.

JOLLY BUTCHER A beerhouse on King Street next to the Generous Briton.

THE RUTLAND ARMS On King Street. This pub was demolished in 2014 to make way for even more car parking.

THE GENEROUS BRITON On King Street.

THE WHEEL This pub closed in 1895; it was on the corner of New Street and King Street.

BRICKLAYERS ARMS This pub on Norman Street closed in the early 2000's.

THE DOG & GUN An alehouse in Pall Mall, it closed in 1909 and the site was used by Farrow's bus garage.

THE ROYAL OAK On Pall Mall, it closed in the 1960's and the area was cleared in 1972.

THE PLASTERER'S ARMS On Bentley street, it closed in about 1980 when the whole area was redeveloped.

THE QUEENS HEAD A short lived Alehouse opposite the Duke of Rutland.

THE DUKE OF RUTLAND On Rutland Street, it closed around 1980 for redevelopment of the area.

THE WOOLPACK On Thorpe End, it closed in the 1870's.

THE WHEATSHEAF This pub stood on Thorpe End and closed in 1983 to allow for road improvements.

THE WHITE HART On Sherrard Street, it closed and became a restaurant in the 21st century but reverted to being a pub.

THE BLACK SWAN On Sherrard Street, the oldest surviving pub on the street it has a carved stone swan outside.

THE THREE CROWNS On Sherrard St.

THE PEACOCK On Sherrard St.

THE MALT SHOVEL On Sherrard St.

THE MARQUIS OF GRANBY INN On Sherrard St, closed in 1936. The building was sixteenth century.

BISHOP BLAIZE On Sherrard St, it closed in 1964. and was demolished The building was fourteenth century.

COACHING HOTELS.

THE GEORGE HOTEL Opened on High Street in the 1700's, it closed early in the 21st century. This was the oldest and most important of the coaching inns and was originally called the George & Talbot'. The building was refurbished during early 2015 for redevelopment after standing empty for some years.

THE BELL HOTEL On Nottingham Street close to the Market Place, the Bell was converted into a shopping arcade after closure in the 1980's, only the façade remaining.

THE HARBOROUGH HOTEL On Burton Street, the last of the old coaching inns to remain open as a hotel. It was named after the Earl of Harborough from Stapleford Hall.

Sherrard Street around 1900, with the Black Swan on the right and the Bishop Blaize on the left….further down on the right is the White Hart.

The Bishop Blaize was an old pub; the building was medieval and the name varied. In 1846 it was the Old Bishop Blaize, then the Bishop Blaize Inn, and by 1877 it was simply the Bishop Blaize. It was named after the patron saint of Woolcombers. It was demolished in 1964, another of Melton's historic buildings that is no longer with us.

Whites 1877 Directory gives an insight into the breweries and pubs in the town:

George Adcock (trustees of) Ale and Porter brewers, Nottingham St and Thorpe End.

Adcock, Pacey & Co. Ale & Porter brewers and maltsters, Eggerton Brewery, Bentley St and Nottingham St. Also Wine & Spirits merchants, Market Place. William Adcock of this firm lived at North Lodge, Bentley St, and James Pacey in Sherrard St.

Thomas Pickard Adcock, Whissendine Brewery Co, & Wine, Spirits & Porter merchant, King St.

Henry Ellingworth, Brewers agent, Thorpe end.   John Fast, Brewer, Whissendine Brewing Co, Cheapside.

William Percy, cooper, Nottingham St…..you can't have beer without barrels!

Angus John, Victualler, Half Moon Inn, Nottingham St.   Samuel Ash, Grocer, Ale & Porter merchant, Burton St.

Mrs Matilda Bailey, Victualler, Black Horse, King St.   Mrs Adelaide Beeby, Victualler, White Lion Hotel.

Mrs Elizabeth Canner, Victualler, Railway Inn, Burton St.   Charles Cawthorpe, Victualler, Golden Fleece, Leicester St.

Alfred Childs, Victualler, George Hotel.   Joseph Clemenston, Victualler, Three Crowns Sherrard St.

James Bolderson, Victualler, King's Head, Nottingham St.   Charles Curtis, Victualler, Eight Bells., Nottingham St.

John Dale, Victualler, Harborough Hotel.   Matthew Dewey, Victualler, Black Swan, Sherrard St.

Thomas Cooke Victualler, Fox Inn, Leicester St.

Mrs Hannah Cotton, Victualler, Generous Briton, King St.

George Gent, Beerhouse, Bentley St.

Richard Goodacre, Victualler, Crown Inn, Burton St.

John Large, Victualler, Blacks Head, Market Place.

William Leake, Wine merchant, Church St.

Josiah Hill, Ale & Porter merchant, Burton St.

Joe Hockin, Victualler, Bell & Swan, Cornhill (aslo a brick manufacturer).

Robert Hutton, Victualler, Bishop Blaize Inn, Sherrard St.

John Ireson, Victualler, Wheatsheaf, Thorpe End.

William Newton, Victualler, Malt Shovel Inn, Sherrard St.

Charles Littlewood, beerhouse, Pall Mall.

Mark Littlewood, beerhouse, Rutland St.

Mrs Eliza Robinson, Victualler, Peacock Inn, Sherrard St.

Miss Ellen Peach, Wine & Spirit merchant, Cheapside.

Thomas Turville, beerhouse, King St.

William Turville, beerhouse, Timber Hill.

William Spencer, Victualler, Granby Inn, Sherrard St.

John Sturgess, Victualler, Lord warden, Leicester St.

James Wilson, beerhouse, Pall Mall.

Henry Walker, Victualler, Noels Arms, Burton St.

James Ward, Victualler, Bricklayers Arms, Timber Hill.

The inns were used as a base by the various carriers connecting the town with the surrounding villages, each inn serving a particular village. The carriers generally only operated this service on Tuesdays, market day.

Some pubs seem to have been missed off the Directory; the Boat isn't listed, for instance, and that was certainly open in 1877.

There were three Temperance Halls in the 1877 directory, but they seem to have been fighting a losing battle!

The top end of Burton Street looking from the market place in about 1900, with the Crown Inn on the right. The large sign on the front wall advertised 'Mowbray Ales'.

Closed pubs. Most of the old pubs shown on the Victorian map have been demolished, but some survive.

The Bricklayers Arms.

The Rutland Arms is demolished during 2014 to make even more car parking space.

The Three Tuns in King Street, still displaying the name on the front. The gable plaque says 1898 but in fact this is one of the oldest buildings in the town.

The Golden Fleece, Leicester Street.

The original pub building was thatched.

The Melton Mowbray breweries.

Melton had two large breweries in the nineteenth century and several small ones that didn't last long—with all those pubs it probably needed them!

First of the large concerns was Adcock, Pacey & Co at Egerton brewery, housed in a large brick building close to the Joint station, part of which survives today. The brewery was established in about 1885, but not on this site which was developed in the late 1870's when the railway was built. The brewery closed in 1919 when the firm was taken over by Ind Coope. In 1863 the firm was being run by William & George Adcock.

The second brewery was at Thorpe End and was founded by George Adcock in 1865 suggesting that at a family feud may have brought about the break away concern, as William was still running the Egerton brewery....in 1875 the brewer was George Adcock Junior. The premises at Thorpe End was taken over by Langton & Sons in 1890 and went out of business in 1910. Again the buildings survive, in use as a gymnasium. Langtons served fourteen tied houses in Melton and the nearby villages, brewing the then well known 'Celebrated AK Ale'.

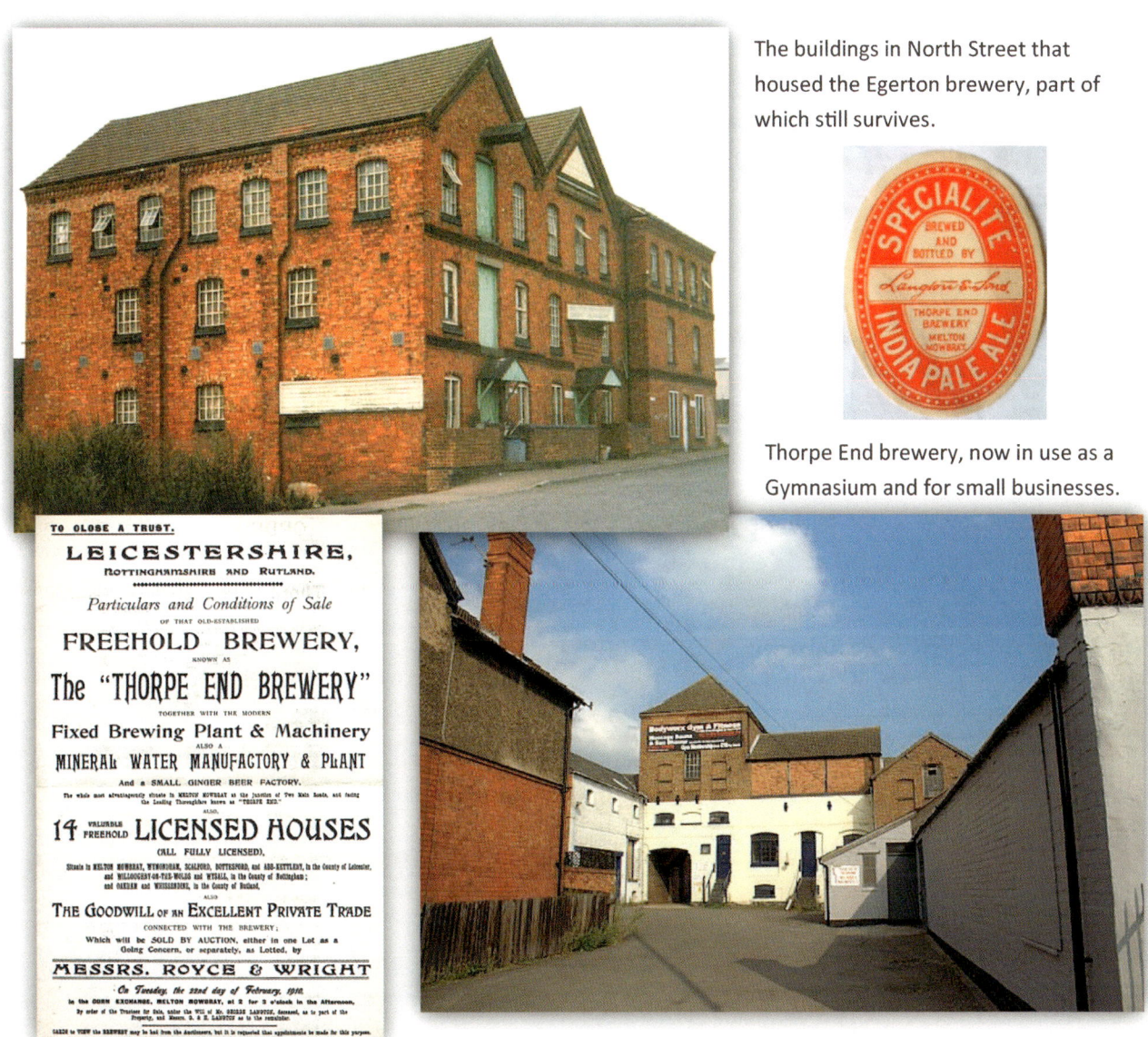

The buildings in North Street that housed the Egerton brewery, part of which still survives.

Thorpe End brewery, now in use as a Gymnasium and for small businesses.

PUBS IN 2015

THE MASH TUB A Marstons pub, it sells two real ales.

THE KINGS HEAD Also a Marstons pub.

THE WHITE LION Owned by Punch Taverns, two real ales are served.

THE HALF MOON Draught Bass is on sale in this town centre pub close to the market square.

THE KETTEBY CROSS Opened by Wetherspoons in a new building in 2009, the pub caught fire in 2010 and was closed for a year for rebuilding. It is now a busy and popular destination. It is named after the market cross that stood at the junction of Leicester Road and Dalby road.

THE FOX The Fox is the oldest pub still in the town centre, but in 2015 it has sadly closed.

THE GRAPES Formerly the tap room of the Swan Inn.

THE CUTTING ROOM Utilising part of the cinema building, the Cutting Room is owed by the Smith & Jones chain; three real ales are served.

THE GENEROUS BRITON A popular live music venue, the Genny B has one real ale.

THE CROWN An Everards pub, the Crown stands just off the market square and serves meals.

THE ANNE OF CLEVES Owned by Everards Brewery, the Anne of Cleves is housed in the oldest building in town after the church and serves meals.

THE NOELS ARMS A free house specialising in live music, and home to the Gasdog brewery. Melton CAMRA pub of the year in 2014, it also sells real cider.

THE HARBOROUGH Still a hotel, it was refurbished during 2014 and sells real ale and cider.

THE BOAT   A free house with four real ales, the Boat retains the atmosphere of a canal side pub despite the water having disappeared in 1877! A former CAMRA pub of the year, it is a friendly and welcoming place for a drink.

THE BLACK SWAN Three real ales are sold.

THE WHITE HART Another occasional music venue, the pub sells two commonly found real ales.

There are also two pubs outside the town centre:

THE CHERRY TREE On Valley Road, it was built when the surrounding houses were erected in the 1970's. Owned by the 'Sizzling' chain it served two real ales. And inexpensive meals.

THE WELBY On Nottingham Road, this one dates from the 1950's when the area was developed. It is owned by Green King who took over after a period of closure, part of their 'Hungry Horse' chain.

Four pubs that thankfully have survived; The Anne of Cleves, The Grapes, The Generous Briton and the Noels Arms.

CHAPTER 15

INDUSTRY.

Melton is by no means an industrial town but a surprising number of businesses have been based here, with many of them still flourishing. This directory dated 1828 reproduced earlier shows how much business there was, built it was all small scale. Large concerns did not begin to appear until the second half of the nineteenth century, and the arrival of the railway in 1846 had a lot to with it.

For a firm to grow beyond being a purely local concern it needed e workforce, to be able to bring in raw materials and to be able to ship out he finished product. It might also need coal for steam powered machinery, to be able to bring in that machinery from the manufacturers, and to be able to source the basic materials for building the works in the first place. All those things were made possible once the railway opened.

This chapter will describe and illustrate the major firms that have been based in Melton since that time.

WYVERN MILLS

The Wyvern Woollen Mill was built on the site of the old water mill adjacent to Scalford Brook. An attempt had been made to open a framework knitting shop in Park Lane in 1793 but it was unsuccessful. The building remains behind the Church, the large windows betraying the industrial use for which it was first erected.

A small scale enterprise of this sort was typical of the time, but by the late 19th century things were being done on a far larger scale. In 1896 the Wyvern Mill was constructed, three storeys high and adjacent to the river to give a water supply for the steam engines powering the machinery. It was built by T.J. Rust & Co. who already had mills elsewhere all operating under the Wyvern name.

The mill was a success and employed hundreds of local women, from the villages as well as the town. It produced a heavy Worsted cloth still knows as Melton cloth; it was closely woven and was waterproof.

The mill continued in production until 1951, latterly producing sewing thread, when the site was sold to Chappie Ltd. They expanded their pet food production and outgrew the mill premises, which was demolished to be replaced by a purpose built factory.

Wyvern Terrace remains as a reminder of the mill, and a few remnants of the buildings can still be seen along the footpath that skirts the Scalford brook.

An aerial view of the mill is included in chapter 2.

CHAPPIE Ltd & PEDIGREE PETFOODS.

The takeover of the Wyvern Mill inn 1951 by Chappie Ltd meant that production continued on the site, but it changed from cloth to petfood and the old mill buildings were soon replaced with purpose built structures.

Mars Ltd, part of the American confectionary empire, had been based in Slough since 1932 and acquired a Manchester based frim called Chappel Brothers. They produced a low priced dog food called 'Chappie'.

Sales of this reached a million pounds in 1951 and a new factory was required to keep up with demand. The company moved production to Melton and by 1953 was working seven days a week, 24 hours a day on a shift system. New brands, Pal and Lassie, were introduced in the 1950's, and now that more than just Chappie was being produced a change of name was required. Petfoods Ltd came intro being in 1956, to be followed by Pedigree Petfoods in 1972. It became the Petfoods division of Mars Ltd in 1975, and by the end of the 1970's three million cans a day were being produced at Melton. The raw materials were brought in from Ascot, and then processed on site.

Cat food brands Whiskas and Kitekat were now being produced as well. The products are the market leaders in the UK, and the factory continued to expand, with the headquarters moving to Waltham on the Wolds.

A railway siding still runs into the works but it is now unused, the relic of an attempt to use rail transport in the 1990's which came to nothing.

THE MIDLAND WOODWORKING COMPANY.

The opening of the Joint railway across the north of Melton in 1879 opened new opportunities for business development. The Midland Woodworking Co. was established close to the joint station on Snow Hill in the 1920's when that part of the town was still open ground. The company was run by Ernest Bailey, and specialised in making stairs and window frames. The firm grew to be a major employer and also got very involved in the social life of the town.

The firm remained independent until 1941 when they were taken over by Boulton & Paul of Norwich. Wooden products for the war effort were produced in the factory, including noses for the gliders used for the D day landings and at Arnhem, prefabricated huts and army bunk beds!

After the war production of window frames and stairs resumed, with a large contract fitting out council houses. The work was less specialised, but in the difficult economic climate anything was welcome. Though part of Boulton & Paul the firm was still family run, with Ernest's son Frank the director until the early 1960's.

In the 1960's a major fire damage part of the works and a garage containing the firms lorries.

The company is now part of JeldWen, and American firm specialising in wooden products. The name came into use in 1999, replacing Rugby Joinery which had absorbed Boulton & Paul and John Carr Timber. There are five UK factories, the Melton one an important part of the business now specialising in stairs and components for windows, doors & door frames for assembly elsewhere.

It seems likely that Mr Bailey commissioned the aerial photographs taken in 1936, as a great many of them show the works on Snowhill. If so, we owe him a debt of thanks!

*Photo courtesy of English Heri*tage.

The joinery works looking east with the Joint station on the right in 1936. The houses in the foreground look to be newly built.

Below, the pond is a relic of the brickworks that stood here, the pond filling the old clay pit.

Staff at the Midland Woodworking Co. in the 1920's, soon after the works opened. It was an important local employer, especially through the depression years of the 1930's.

A lorry owned by Midland Woodworking at the garage on Snowhill in about 1935 which maintained the fleet and was a subsidiary of the firm.

THE MELTON MOWBRAY GAS LIGHT & COKE COMPANY

At one time every town had a gas works, but the advent of gas from the North Sea in the 1970's saw the rapid demise of those that had survived that long. Melton gasworks closed in the early 1950's when the Pedigree factory spread across the site so that nothing now remains of it.

The gas company was formed on 7th June 1834 and the gas works built on Occupation Road (Regent Road and Brook Street were later additions). The company remained independent until 1937 when it was absorbed by Gas Consolidation Ltd, and this was in turn nationalised in 1949.

Melton gas works was not connected to the railway with a siding, but it was only a short distance from the station to which coal would be delivered. This was a small works, but quite large enough to serve the town. The single gasometer had 'MELTON MOWBRAY' painted on the domed top in the twentieth century, and one can imagine that being hastily painted out in 1939. The company offices were in High Street.

The product was referred to as 'Coal Gas' or 'Town Gas'.

MELTON MOWBRAY ELECTRIC LIGHT COMPANY

This enterprise opened a generating station with an address on the north side of Mill Street on September 15th 1899, supplying power to the town and for street lighting in direct competition with the gas company. It remained independent until nationalisation in 1948.

The Electricity works is the building with the tall chimney on the right of this picture; it is actually on Regent Street rather than Mill Street. The premises is now a garage, and other than the chimney remains much as built.

The gas works in 1938, with the town name clearly painted on top of the gasometer. Access to the works was from the corner of Brook Street and Regent Street, seen bottom left.

Wyvern Mill can be seen beyond the gasworks; this entire site is now occupied by the Pedigree factory which stretches as far as Burton Road railway bridge. Scalford Brook runs in front of the mill. The houses on the left side of Regent Street have been demolished.

This is the site today; other than the Scalford brook it is unrecognisable, flanked on both sides by the new buildings of the Pedigree factory. In earlier times this was the site of a medieval water mill.

This is the generating station erected by the Electric Light Company, now in use as Wilson's garage. The chimney has been felled but other than that the buildings remain very original.

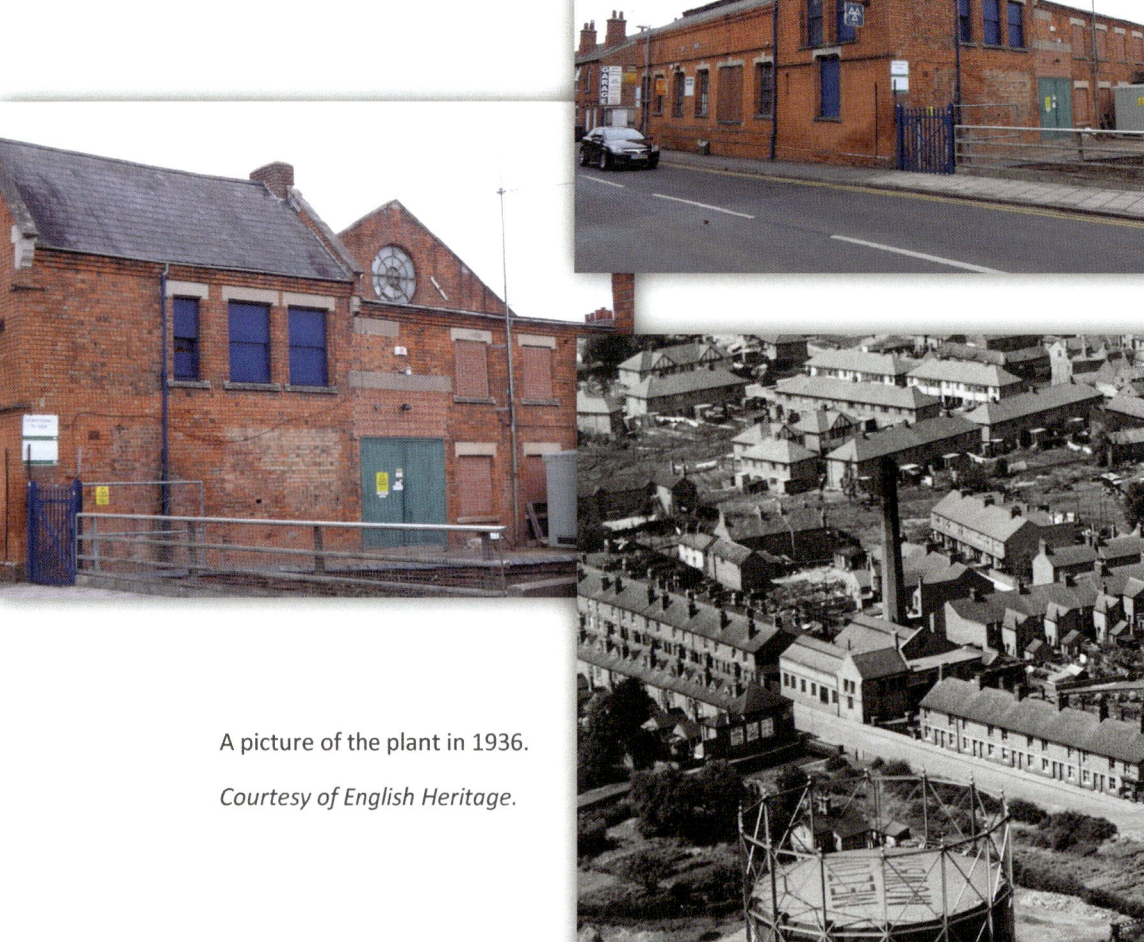

A picture of the plant in 1936.

Courtesy of English Heritage.

Ministry of Fuel and Power—1947.

MELTON MOWBRAY (CAPITAL POWERS) ORDER, 1947.

(APPLICATION FOR AN ORDER UNDER SECTION 1 OF THE GAS UNDERTAKINGS ACT, 1929.)

NOTICE is hereby given that the Melton Mowbray Gas Light and Coke Company Limited (hereinafter called " the Company ") whose address is High Street Melton Mowbray in the county of Leicester, intend to apply to the Minister of Fuel and Power for an Order under Section 1 of the Gas Undertakings Act, 1929, for the following purposes (that is to say):—

(1) To authorise the Company to raise at any time during a period of three years after the date on which the Order comes into effect additional share capital not exceeding £20,000.

(2) To authorise the Company to borrow on mortgage of their gas undertaking or by the creation and issue of debenture stock money not exceeding in the whole the aggregate amount of the paid-up share capital for the time being of the Company for the purposes of such undertaking and of any premiums paid in respect thereof.

(3) To modify the provisions of Section 7 of the Melton Mowbray Gas Order, 1889, and Sections 9 and 11 of the Melton Mowbray Gas Order, 1915, and to repeal or amend any other provisions of the Melton Mowbray Gas Orders, 1889 to 1923.

and of any other Act or Order affecting the Company as may be necessary in order to give full effect to the proposed Order.

Any local or other public authority, company or person desiring to bring before the Minister of Fuel and Power any objection to the application may do so by registered letter addressed to the Minister and despatched on or before the 7th day of June, 1947.

Any such objection must state the specific grounds of objection and a copy of the objection must be forwarded to the under-mentioned Solicitor at the same time as it is sent to the Minister.

Dated this 7th day of May, 1947.

R. H. STUDHOLME, Solicitor, 15, Moorgate, (317) London, E.C.2.

_____

CHAPTER 16

PORK PIES AND STILTON CHEESE

The two words Melton Mowbray are famous the world over for preceding two more words, pork pie! People may have no idea where Melton is, but they know all about a Melton Mowbray pork pie. They will have heard of Stilton Cheese too, though in that case they may not associate it with Melton. Both delicacies, though, owe their fame to our town.

STILTON CHEESE.

At one time almost every farm made cheese; it was easier to make your own on the spot, like brewing beer. Each locality had it's distinctive types, and while some died out others became nationally known brands. Everyone knows that Cheddar Cheese originated in Somerset; not everyone realises that Stilton cheese originated in Melton Mowbray.

Stilton is a blue cheese with a strong taste and aroma; there is a white version too, but it is blue Stilton that you immediately think of when you hear the name. It is a protected name now, and only cheese manufactured in Leicestershire, Derbyshire or Nottinghamshire can call itself Stilton. The name is distracting, because the village of Stilton lies in Huntingdonshire on the Great North Road, now the A1. In Stilton was an inn called The Bell, and in 1730 it was owned by Cooper Thornhill, an enterprising gentleman. He paid a visit during 1730 to a farm close to Melton, possibly in Wymondham, possibly to visit relatives. On the farm they made the local cheese, as all the farms around did, for their own use and to sell at Melton market. The farmers wife was called Frances Pawlett, so perhaps she should be given the credit for inventing Stilton.

Cooper Thornhill was very taken with this cheese, so when he returned home he took some with him to serve to his guests at the inn. Being on the Great North Road it was a busy establishment, and the cheese immediately became very popular with the travellers. He realised he was onto a good thing so he made an agreement with the farmer that he would only sell his cheese to the Bell for exclusive use. Wagon loads were soon being delivered the thirty miles from Wymondham, and of course the travellers, not knowing where the cheese originated, just referred to it as the 'cheese from Stilton', or Stilton cheese. The name stuck.

It's a good story, and like all good stories it certainly contains some truth, but in fact the first written reference to Stilton Cheese came years before, in 1722 when William Stuckeley wrote a letter mentioning it, as did Daniel Defoe two years later. He described Stilton as 'a town famous for its cheese', but whether this was a different cheese in those days isn't clear. A recipe for Stilton cheese was published in 1726 when it was said to be produced at the Bell Inn itself, suggesting that the cheese they were describing was a very different item.

I think we can accept that though cheese was made and sold in Stilton long before 1730, what we know as Stilton Cheese today originated on that farm in Wymondham.

The Bell Inn was rather more than a roadside pub, it was a proper coaching inn with accommodation and stables for changing the horses on stage coaches.

Happily the Inn remains open today, and yes, it still serves Stilton Cheese. The building dates from 1642, though an inn was on the site at least as far back as 1500. Enlargement work done in 1736 resulted in the present building, just after our cheese arrived on the scene.

Stilton is a blue cheese, the distinctive veins being formed by piercing he cheese with steel needles which allows air into the centre of the cheese. To mature a Stilton takes between nine and twelve weeks.

At the time of writing only six dairies manufacture Stilton, three in Leicestershire, two in Nottinghamshire and one in Derbyshire. Four of them are in the Vale of Belvoir close to Melton Mowbray.

To be called a Stilton, the cheese must, apart from having the blue veins, have a cylindrical shape, form its own crust, be unpressed and 'have the typical Stilton taste profile'. There are similar cheese, of course, and many are produced in the same or a very similar way, but they all have to be called something else that could not be confused with Stilton.

Tuxford and Tebbutt's creamery at Thorpe End in Melton is keeping the tradition going in the town, and has been doing so for many years. Tebbutt & Crosher began as a pork pie maker in 1867 and later took as a partner in the firm William Thorpe Tuxford who was already a Stilton cheese factor. Stilton cheese production began in 1909; the pies were traded separately until 1928 when the company became one. As the years passed cheese production became increasingly important and the bakery side of the business ended in 1966 to allow for an expansion of the cheese making.

They also make Red Leicester cheese nowadays, but the less said about that the better!

PORK PIES

The pork pie wasn't created in Melton Mowbray; people have been eating pork pies for almost as long as they've been eating pork, and as the pig was the first farm animal to be domesticated that is many tens of thousands of years.

What did happen first in Melton, though, is that pork pie manufacture became commercialised.

As with Stilton Cheese, every farmers wife would make pork pies. A pig was a prized possession of every cottage dweller, to be fattened over the summer and killed in the Autumn to provide the family with food through the winter. Only when people began to live in towns in large numbers did this practice begin to die out, and even then a pig in the back yard wasn't unknown. Butchers shops took the place of each family having a pig and so the selling of meat became more organised, leading to the selling of meat products such as pork pies.

The first enterprising baker to produce the pies on a large scale was Edward Adcock but he was certainly not the first to make and sell them, that has been happening for years. As far back as the 1790 William Easom began a bakery business producing pies and confectionary on the Beast Market, now Sherrard Street, and he probably deserves the credit for beginning the process. The shop was moved to Butcher's Row, (Cheapside), and the business continued to trade until the 1960's, the bakery itself being on Thorpe End. The pies produced by Mr Easom, though, were for local consumption and produced in smallish quantities as required by a single shop.

Edward Adcock had bigger ideas; he wanted to sell pork pies in London!

His bakehouse was in a yard alongside the Fox Inn, which can still be seen. Edwards father ran a confectionery shop in Nottingham Street, and trade increased through the early 1800's after the introduction of the London to Leeds mail coach which stopped at Melton overnight. He delivered his products to be sold in London by using the coach for transport, and Edward though the same could be done with pork pies. He was right, and by 1849 he had moved to larger premises on Burton End. His son in law William Taylor had a bakery in Leicester and when Edward grew older Taylors took over the whole business....by 1895 they were the largest pork pie makers in Leicester.

The Fox Inn on Leicester Street, once a stopping place for coaches which would draw into the yard through the opening to the left of the inn. The bakehouse of Edward Adcock was also through the opening in the rear yard of the inn.

This is one of the few rows of buildings in Melton that would have looked very similar in the 1830's.

The pork pies from Adcocks bakehouse were taken to London in boxes strapped to the top of the stage-coach, beginning in about 1830, and the product soon became fashionable and sought after. This is when the name of the town became connected with the pie, in the same way as happened with Stilton Cheese.

In the 1830's there were seven businesses producing pies in Melton, but only Adcock had the initiative to look outside the town for his market and the happy chance that Melton lay on the route of the coach to London made his enterprise possible.

In 1848 a well known name enters the picture; John Dickinson opened a new bakehouse on Burton End to produce pies. He must have done well because in 1851 he leased a second bakehouse on Nottingham Street and that is where Dickinson and Morris shop has been ever since. The production of pies was given a boost when the railway opened, meaning that the pies to could be got to London and other large cities much more quickly and in larger quantities. The stage coach made the industry possible; the railway finally made it possible to produce pies on an industrial scale. A new bakehouse was opened on Burton Street in 1860 and the proximity to the station was not a coincidence.

Dickinson and Morris was bought by Samworth Brothers in 1992, ensuring a healthy future for the business.

It was not Dickinson and Morris, though, that were responsible for the huge expansion of interest in the pies in the 1880's, and for the cementing of their reputation as a product of the highest quality. Enoch Evans had a pie factory on Sherrard Street in 1840 and business was so good that by 1855 he couldn't meet the huge demand. He decided to construct a purpose built factory at Thorpe End which opened in 1860, and the smaller bakery was sold. His nephew James Hill joined the company, now renamed Evans & Hill. The company boasted in their advertising that they were the *'Original manufacturers of the celebrated Melton Mowbray pork, veal and ham and game pies'.* The company received a boost when an American writer, Elihu Burritt, visited the town in 1863, had a tour of the factory, and wrote in glowing terms about the pies when he got home. Soon they were being shipped to the USA aboard the new Transatlantic steam ships, another case of a new technology coming along at the right time to help the business expand into new areas.

Burritt visited the town again in 1867 and this was reported in the Daily Telegraph, all good free advertising!

Evans and Hill traded until 1910 when it was purchased by Henry Morris, a cheese manufacturer. It made sense to make both products under the same roof as they were so closely related. In 1892 the works employed forty people on pie making alone.

The factory closed in 1952 ands sadly it was demolished for road widening in 1963. The site is mostly occupied by Morrisons supermarket.

Sherrard Street in 1926; the pork pie factory is arrowed. You can see why it was demolished to allow the street to be straightened!

There were other pork pie makers in the town, notable Warners in the market place, Tuxfords and Henry Colins & Co, the latter two the only other companies who were catering for the mass market.

Colin began his bakery in 1860 on Burton End, convenient for the station, and in 1881 built a larger premises. They factored Stilton as well as making pies, which means that the cheese was bought from the surrounding area, usually the farms, to be sent on to London and other destinations by train. The pies had an excellent reputation; in 1868 they provided 5000 pies for the Leicester Agricultural show!

The company was hit hard by the First World War and was bought by Evans & Co. in 1919, the bakery being closed.

The last of the big three pie-makers in the town were Tuxfords, who began production in 1867 having built a factory in Thorpe End. The frim was begun by Mr Tebbutt & Mr Crosher who had been gentlemen's outfitters—it was quite a change in occupation! Mr Crosher disappears from the story early on and William Tuxford joined them in partnership, already having a thriving Stilton factoring business. The two firms used the same factory, and began actually producing cheese themselves in 1909. The name was changed to that it carries today in 1928, Tuxford & Tebbutt Ltd. The firm finished making pies in 1966 to concentrate just on cheese.

CHAPTER 17

LEISURE.

For most people leisure is a fairly recent concept; until the twentieth century paid holidays were unknown and small towns provided few facilities other than public houses. Working people worked long hours for little money, and while a walk in the park on a Sunday was free and could be enjoyed by everyone other pastimes tended to be confined to the better off. The other limiting factor was the lack of artificial light until gas lighting was introduced, which made large gatherings difficult after dark.

However, gradually leisure facilities began to be introduced in Melton and today it is very fortunate in the variety on offer for such a small place.

THE PARKS

The visitor to Melton cannot help but notice the large expanses of parkland in the town, mainly the south and west of the town centre. The existence of the Town Estate has been a huge factor in this but it is worth considering how the parks were acquired piecemeal over the years.

The parks comprise Play Close, Priors Close, New Park, Wilton Park and Egerton Park.

PLAY CLOSE. The first park to be developed was Play Close which was bought for £170 by the Town Estate in 1866, but it has been used for the town fair since at least 1848 and the townspeople considered it to be common land. Lord Melbourne's agents built pigsties on it and provoked the 'Play Close Riots' in 1848, the offending buildings quickly being removed. To prevent anything similar happening again, in 1850 the land was bought for the town by Mr T. Ward and Mr W. Tuxford, on the understanding that it would be bought from them by the town estate when funds permitted; in the event it took sixteen years to raise the money.

Further smaller pieces of land were bought in 1872 and 1886 to enlarge the park, bringing it to the size we know today.

Play Close has been the home of the annual Melton Mowbray Show since 1983. A postcard dated 1911 shows sheep grazing on the park in order to keep the grass short, an economical alternative to mowing it.

PRIORS CLOSE This area was presented to the town in 1985 by Mrs Audrey Mars, wife of the founder of the company Forrest mars. It covers the area of the former allotments which had become overgrown a derelict, and eyesore that could clearly be seen from the station and from Play Close. The presentation marked the 50th anniversary of Pedigree Petfoods. The new area borders Play Close and the route of the old canal was marked where the parks meet.

NEW PARK This park was opened in 1909 by Mr Henry Wood who had laid out the park in his position as Townwarden. The bandstand is the main feature of New Park, which survives very much in original condition.

The park has iron gates leading onto the bottom end of Leicester Street.

The view across Play Close towards the Church.

WILTON PARK. This facility is aimed at the more active, with tennis courts, a bowling green, a playground, a miniature railway, a pitch and putt course and a Café. It was an open field and was bought from Lady Wilton in 1919, it being felt that in the aftermath of the Great War it would beneficial to give the town a new leisure area. The cost of the purchase was £400, and conversion into a park began at once, with the emphasis very much on providing sports facilities.

EGERTON PARK The final addition was Egerton Park, bought in 1931 for £1400 in order to provide football, cricket and hockey pitches.

EGERTON LODGE MEMORIAL GARDENS Not part of the parks, but complementary to them, the gardens were bought for £500 in 1929 following he death of Lady Wilton, filling the area between Egerton Lodge and the river. Eighteenth century yew trees are a feature of the gardens as are the memorials to the two world wars. The gardens were from the start intended as a place for quiet reflection, something not readily possible in the more open parks already in use.

S 10377   THE RIVER AND PARK, MELTON MOWBRAY.

This postcard shows New Park soon after it opened.

The parks have long been a meeting place for local hunts.

THE CINEMAS.

I have used the plural because there have been two cinemas in the town. Remarkably, both were in King Street.

The Picture House was opened in 1920, and by 1926 it was operated by George Scarborough. In 1930 a British Thomson Houston(BTH) sound system was installed. In 1933 George Scarborough built the Regal Cinema adjacent to the Picture House.

The Picture House was re-named Plaza Cinema in 1939, when it offered live shows as well as films. The Plaza Cinema and the Regal Cinema were both later operated by the Evington Cinema Circuit.

The Plaza Cinema was closed in 1962 and was converted into a bingo club. The bingo club was closed in 1974, and moved next door to the Regal Cinema building. The Plaza Cinema stood unused until it was demolished in 1982 and the site is now occupied by St. Mary's Way.

THE REGAL

The Regal Cinema was once described by Made in Dagenham writer William Ivory as the "finest cinema in England". The cinema was run by John Merryweather from the year 2000 as a labour of love but the future of the enterprise was thrown into doubt when he died in 2012. Happily a campaign to save the cinema was launched and the future is now secure, with the Regal being run by a family who also own a small cinema in Belper. Few towns as small as Melton are lucky enough to have kept their cinema, and in such original condition too. The only major alteration has been the opening of the Cutting Room pub in rooms no longer required beneath the building.

THE MELTON THEATRE.

The first theatre in Melton was the Palace on Leicester Street which in 1913 was also showing films.

The present theatre opened in 1976, funded mainly by Pedigree Petfoods, and it is a remarkable facility for a small town, the auditorium having more than 300 seats.

In late 2014 it was refurbished with a modern extension on the site formerly used by the bus garage.

The original theatre building is on the right; the very dark brick used for the walls make it a sombre looking building. On the left is the new section opened in 2014 which is much lighter and more attractive.

THE GREYHOUND STADIUM.

This was located on Saxby Road and opened on 11th June 1949; it closed in 1969 and the site is now covered by an industrial estate. Speedway meetings were also held there for which the track was covered with matting.

THE SWIMMING BATHS

Standing at the bottom of Dalby Road the Waterfields baths opened in 1965 with an indoor pool, learner pool and gymnasium. There had formerly been a paddling pool in Play Close and an open air swimming pool off Saxby Road but that was closed and filled in. The new building was funded by public donations, an impressive achievement for a small town. The extension to the pool housing the flume was added in the 1990's.

CHAPTER 18

MODERN MELTON

To finish the book are some pictures of modern Melton, good and bad, on the basis that what is commonplace today will be history tomorrow.

In 2011 the town had a population of 27,158 and covered a vastly expanded area compared to that shown on the Victorian maps, most it housing constructed since 1945.

At the time of writing the newest building in town is the Premier Inn which opened at the beginning of 2015. This is the modern equivalent of the coaching inns of old, fulfilling the same function.

Much less pleasing is the wasteland that was Charlotte Street, a community of Victorian houses torn down around 1980 and replace with...this!

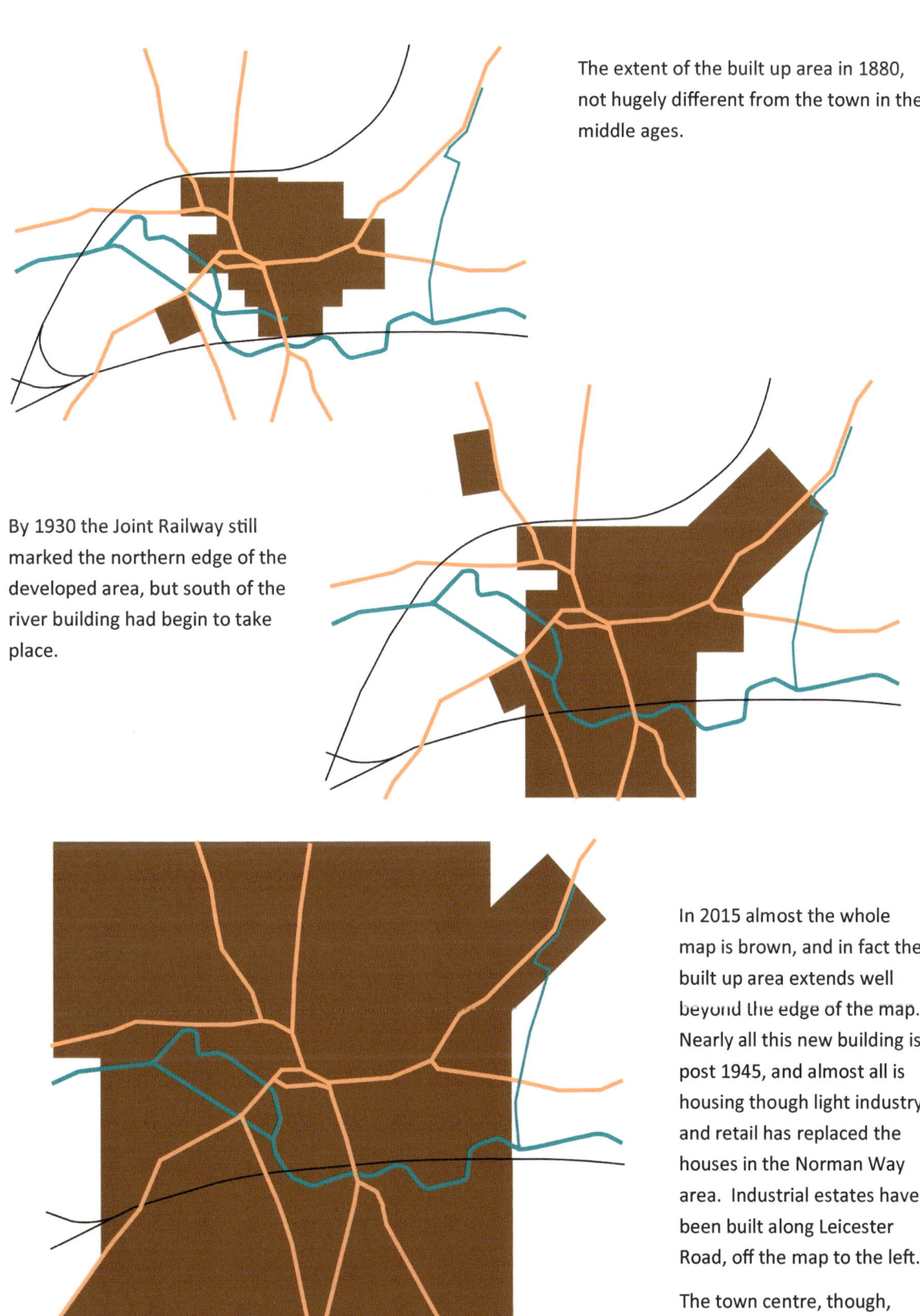

The extent of the built up area in 1880, not hugely different from the town in the middle ages.

By 1930 the Joint Railway still marked the northern edge of the developed area, but south of the river building had begin to take place.

In 2015 almost the whole map is brown, and in fact the built up area extends well beyond the edge of the map. Nearly all this new building is post 1945, and almost all is housing though light industry and retail has replaced the houses in the Norman Way area. Industrial estates have been built along Leicester Road, off the map to the left.

The town centre, though, would still be recognisable to a visitor from 1880.

Tranquil corners can still be found, and even on this March day it was warm enough to sit and enjoy the parks.

This is the cemetery behind Chapel street.

The old garage on the corner of Wilton Road and High Street was no longer required as a garage so has been very cleverly turned into a supermarket while retaining the 1930's look to the architecture. An example of how it should be done.

The Bell Hotel in 1960.

By the early 1980's the Hotel had closed but rather than demolish it the façade was retained and a shopping arcade built behind it—another pat on the back, it's an excellent development but sadly many of the shops are currently empty. The centre is owned by the Co-op.

What a shame the same flair seems to have failed elsewhere in the town; I find these areas profoundly depressing.

The Victorians know how to do this well, with houses, shops and pubs all mixed in.

Sometimes I wonder if planners should be forced to live in the areas they create.

Something more cheering to finish on; the pedestrianisation of much of the town centre has been a great success as seen here in historic King Street. There's no one about because it was early on Sunday morning; usually it's bustling.

LISTED BUILDINGS IN MELTON MOWBRAY

Despite the demolitions of the past that have robbed us of so much, Melton still has a surprising number of listed buildings.

1 SOUTH PARADE   GRADE 2

1-3 LEICESTER YARD   GRADE 2

1-7 LEICESTER STREET GRADE 2

10 HIGH STREET GRADE 2

10 MARKET PLACE GRADE 2

11 & 11A NOTTINGHAM STREET GRADE 2

11 & 12 MARKET PALCE GRADE 2

11 & 13 SCALFORD ROAD   GRADE 2

11 & 13 BURTON STREET   GRADE 2

11 & 13 LEICESTER ROAD   GRADE 2

12 & 14 CHURCH STREET   GRADE 2

12 HIGH STREET GRADE 2

13 7 23 NORMAN WAY   GRADE 2

13 MARKET PLACE GRADE 2

14 & 15 MARKET PLACE GRADE 2

14 BURTON STREET   GRADE 2

15 BROOK LANE   GRADE 2

15 HIGH STREET   GRADE 2

15 LEICESTER ROAD   GRADE 2

16, A606   GRADE DL

16 CHURCH STREET   GRADE 2

16 MARKET PLACE GRADE

17, A606   GRADE DL

17 BROOK LANE   GRADE 2

17 LEICESTER ROAD   GRADE 2

18 CHURCH STREET V GRADE 2

19 LEICESTER ROAD   GRADE 2

2 CHURCH TERRACE   GRADE 2

2 SOUTH PARADE   GRADE 2

20 & 22 PARK ROAD   GRADE 2

25 BURTON STREET   GRADE 2

26 MARKET PLACE GRADE 2

27 BURTON STREET   GRADE 2

27 LEICESTER ROAD   GRADE C2

27 MARKET PLACE   GRADE 2

29 AND 29A MARKET PLACE GRADE 2

3 & 11 SAGE CROSS STREET GRADE 2

3 CHURCH TERRACE GRADE 2

3 KING STREET GRADE 2

3 TO 5 SOUTH PARADE GRADE 2

30, 30A AND 32 MARKET PLACE GRADE 2

32 7 34 PARK ROAD   GRADE 2

33 & 35 BURTON STREET   GRADE 2

34, 35 & 35A MARKET PLACE GRADE 2

34 DALBY ROAD GRADE 2

37 & 37A NOTTINGHAM STREET GRADE 2

37—41 BURTON STREET GRADE 2

FOUR LAMP POSTS CHURCH TERRACE GRADE 2

4 HIGH STREET GRADE 2

4 NOTTINGHAM STREET GRADE 2

43-47 BURTON STREET GRADE 2

44 7 46 SHERRARD STREET GRADE 2

5 CHURCH TERRACE GRADE 2

5 KING STREET GRADE 2

54 & 44 THORPE END GRADE 2

6 CHURCH TERRACE GRADE 2

6 SOUTH PARADE GRADE 2

64 SHERRARD STREET GRADE 2

7 BURTON STREET GRADE 2

7 CHURCH TERRACE GRADE 2

8 & 8A BURTON STREET GRADE 2

9 NORMAN WAY GRADE 2

9, 11 & 11A HIGH STREET GRADE 2

9 BURTON STREET GRADE 2

PARTS OF THE WAR MEMORIAL HOSPITAL ANKLE HILL GRADE 2

ANNE OF CLEVES BURTON STREET GRADE 2*

ARCHWAY, EGERTON LODGE, GRADE 2

BANDSTAND, NEW PARK GRADE 2

BAPTIST CHAPEL NOTTINGHAM ST GRADE 2

BARN AT RIVERSIDE VIEW GRADE 2

BELL HOTEL FACADE GRADE 2

CANAL BRIDGE, LEICESTER ROAD GRADE 2

CARDIGAN HOUSE GRADE 2

CENTRAL METHODIST CHURCH SAGE CROSS STREET GRADE DL

CENTRAL BLOCK, ST MARY'S HOSPITAL GRADE 2

CHURCH OF ST MARY. GRADE 2

COACH ARCH, 15 HIGH STREET GRADE 2

COLLES HALL BURTON STREET GRADE 2

CRAVEN LODGE BURTON ROAD GRADE 2

CRAWFORD HOUSE A606 GRADE 2

EGERTON LODGE GRADE 2

ELGIN LODGE GRADE 2

ENTRANCE GATES TO NEW PARK. GRADE 2

FRAMLAND HOUSE GRADE 2

HARBOROUGH HOTEL GRADE 2

HOLMLEIGH PARK LANE GRADE 2

LADY WILTON'S BRIDGE GRADE 2

LATHAM HOUSE GRADE 2

LLOYDS BANK NOTTINGHAM ST GRADE 2

MAGISTRATES COURT GRADE 2

MAISON DIEU BEDEHOUSES GRADE 2

MEMORIAL HOSPITAL GRADE 2

PARISH CHURCH OF ST MARY **GRADE 1**

PROVIDENCE PLACE, MILL LANE GRADE 2

RIVERSIDE COTTAGE & FARMHOUSE GRADE 2

ROMAN CATHOLIC CHURCH OF ST JOHN. G2

ST MARYS INFANTS SCHOOL. GRADE 2

SYSONBY LODGE GRADE 2

THE BOAT INN GRADE 2

THE CORN EXCHANGE GRADE 2

THE CROWN INN GRADE 2

THE FOX INN GRADE 2

THE GEORGE HOTEL GRADE 2

THE GRAPES INN GRADE 2

THE RED HOUSE, NOTTINGHAM STREET   GRADE 2

THE UNITED REFORM CHUCH GRADE 2

THE WHITE LION INN   GRADE 2

YE PORK PIE SHOPPE, NOTTINGHAM STREET GRADE 2*

THE SWAN PORCH GRADE DL

THE WHEATSHEAF INN (DEMOLISHED) G2

TOAD HALL   GRADE 2

BIBLIOGRAPHY AND SOURCES

www.meltonmowbrayrailways.info

www.systonandpeterborough.co.uk

Both run by the author, both these sites give far more information than can be included in this book.

THE MELTON MOWRBAY ALBUM   TREVOR HICKMAN   SUTTON PUBLISHING 1997

THE MELTON MOWBRAY PORK PIE   TREVOR HICKMAN SUTTON PUBLISHING 1997

MELTON MOWBRAY A PHOTGRAPHIC HISTORY SARAH STIRLING & JULIA ELLIS 2002

THE MELTON TO OAKHAM CANAL   DAVID TEW   SYCAMORE PRESS 1984

THE MELTON MOWBRAY NAVIGATION M. MILLER & S. FLETCHER RCHS 1984

THE STORY OF MELTON MOWBRAY PHILIP HUNT   REPRINT PRESS 1977   (ORIGINALLY 1957)

42300050R00082

Made in the USA
Charleston, SC
23 May 2015